Intelli-Shred

The Thinking Guitarist's Guide to Melodic Mastery

Alfred, the leader in educational publishing,

and the National Guitar Workshop,

one of America's finest guitar schools, have joined

forces to bring you the best, most progressive

educational tools possible. We hope you will enjoy

this book and encourage you to look for

other fine products from Alfred and the

National Guitar Workshop.

Alfred Publishing Co., Inc.
16320 Roscoe Blvd., Suite 100
P.O. Box 10003
Van Nuys, CA 91410-0003
alfred.com

ISBN-10: 0-7390-4745-0 (Book & CD)
ISBN-13: 978-0-7390-4745-3 (Book & CD)

This book was acquired, edited and produced
by Workshop Arts, Inc., the publishing arm of
the National Guitar Workshop.
Nathaniel Gunod, acquisitions, managing editor
Burgess Speed, editor
Matthew Liston, assistant editor
Timothy Phelps, interior design
Ante Gelo, music typesetter
CD recorded by Mark Schane-Lydon at WorkshopLive.com, Pittsfield, MA

Cover Photographs
Guitar: courtesy of Jackson® Guitars, USA • Head and brain: © istockphoto.com / angelhell
Explosion: © istockphoto.com / Soubrette • Lightning: © istockphoto.com / nopow

TABLE OF CONTENTS

A compact disc is available with this book. Using the disc will help make learning more enjoyable and the information more meaningful. Listening to the CD will help you correctly interpret the rhythms and feel of each example. The symbol to the left appears next to each example that is performed on the CD. Example numbers are above the symbol. The track number below each symbol corresponds directly to the example you want to hear. In many cases, there is more than one example per track; this is reflected in the track numbers (for example: track 2.1, track 2.2, track 2.3, etc.). Track 1 will help you tune to this CD.

ABOUT THE AUTHOR

Photo by Adam Forrester

Kevin Dillard has over 30 years of experience in the world of music, having started at the age of five. A self-taught guitarist, he adapted piano studies to create his own unique guitar method. He later went on to study music theory, composition and percussion at the University of South Alabama.

In 2001, Kevin was involved in an accident which shattered two vertebrae in his neck, causing spinal trauma that left him paralyzed from the neck down. He was told he would never walk again. However, he began to regain movement only four days after a miraculously successful seven-hour spinal fusion surgery. In less than one year, Kevin was fully functional and had returned to full-time music performance and instruction.

A music instructor for the past 17 years, Kevin teaches guitar, theory and improvisation at Cascade Hills Church (www.cascadehills.com) at the School of the Arts program in Columbus, Georgia. He has served as a mentor for graduation requirements in Columbus High's Mentor Program and has been a speaker at Muscogee County school career day events. Kevin has been involved in promoting children's music education, and in 2003 and 2004, he was one of Georgia's spokesmen for VH1's "Save the Music" program.

Kevin has performed as a clinician at various outlets and events for the some of the biggest names in the music industry and is currently an endorser for DiMarzio guitar pickups and accessories. You can find his soundclips demoing some of their products on their website: www.dimarzio.com. Kevin also currently serves and performs on the television ministry "Realtime with Bill Purvis," reaching a television audience of over 350 million viewers on a weekly basis. There's also a live webcast every Sunday to millions. In the summer, you can study rock guitar with Kevin at the National Guitar Workshop (www.guitarworkshop.com).

Check out the following websites for more on Kevin and the gear he uses:

- www.myspace.com/intellishred
- www.dimarzio.com
- www.intelli-shred.com

ACKNOWLEDGEMENTS

I'd like to thank God for giving me the opportunity to write this book and to play, perform and support my family through music. I'd like to thank my wife Hayley and my children Colton, Devany and Tegan for their love, support, patience and understanding. Thank you to my mom, Betty, for all her years of love and support. A HUGE thanks to David Smolover, Burgess Speed, Nat Gunod and the folks at NGW/Workshop Arts for believing in me as an author, artist and instructor. THANKS to Matt Smith, for without you this would not be possible! Much thanks for your friendship and guidance. Thanks to Steve Blucher at DiMarzio, Jeremy "Jem" Humberstone at Nocturne Guitars, Morley Pedals, DR Handmade Strings, Line 6, and Pickboy/Brooklyn Gear.

INTRODUCTION

Welcome to *Intelli-Shred*. This book explores the often-neglected topic of intelligent melodic development. Most shred guitar teachers focus on two aspects of guitar playing: 1) the mechanical aspects of developing technique, speed and facility; 2) music theory such as scales, chords and arpeggios. The danger of this approach is getting boxed into a pattern of "speed for speed's sake" and sounding mechanical or sterile. The exercises in *Intelli-Shred*, on the other hand, make good melodic sense whether played fast or slow. By understanding the fretboard, you'll be able to pull whatever flavors, moods or colors you want from your guitar, without having to play every note of a scale or mode. Rather than playing more notes at blinding speed, you'll learn to eliminate the unnecessary notes to find the intelligent, melodic choices. *Intelli-Shred* emphasizes the process of melodic discovery, giving you the tools to develop coherent musical ideas of your own.

This book is written with a relaxed and conversational tone and tries to capture the experience of sitting in a room with a good teacher. It's supposed to be a warm and personable experience, not a cold, technical textbook.

Intelli-Shred is not a "learn to play guitar" book. You won't learn how to read music or play barre chords. Rather, it's intended for experienced players looking to take their playing to the next level. If you need a refresher on the basics, check out *The Total Rock Guitarist* by Tobias Hurwitz (Alfred/National Guitar Workshop #24423). If you're unfamiliar with any of the techniques or notations in *Intelli-Shred*, consult the Notation Key on page 95.

Here are some tips on how to approach the material in this book:

1. **Take it slow and easy.** Don't try to work through all of it at once. Give the information and exercises time to sink in. Get each of the shapes, patterns, scales and licks under you fingers before moving on to the next exercise. It may take a little while before you can visualize patterns on the fretboard or before the theory makes sense. Also, information is processed more easily in small amounts and shorter practice sessions, rather than Herculean marathons lasting several hours. You'll retain what you've learned and be able to make better use of it more quickly this way. Unless you're already accustomed to two-hour practice sessions, try 15- to 30-minute bursts instead.

2. **Combine licks and exercises.** Playing up and down the same old scale patterns can get boring; try combining fragments of these licks with others in the book or with your own that you've already worked out. As with any new concept, lick, trick, pattern or scale, once you've got it down, ask yourself, "Now, how can I twist and warp this idea to make it my own?"

Please, for the sake of music: EXPERIMENT! Get creative! Use the ideas in this book as springboards and launching pads for you own musical ideas. Strive to find your own voice on the guitar—your own musical identity. Most prospective students approach their new teacher and ask, "Can you make me play and sound just like (insert the name of their favorite guitarist here)?" But the world already has a Steve Vai, a John Petrucci and a Joe Satriani. What the world really needs is YOU. What do *you* have to say? How will you choose to express your living, breathing creativity with your chosen instrument? What will be your personal musical statement? This attitude will open new doors for you as a guitarist, as an overall musician, and as a unique voice in the world.

PRACTICE VS. JAMMING

Most of us go through peaks and plateaus in our continuing development as players. One of the most beneficial (yet often overlooked) skills is the ability to organize your practice sessions. How do you optimize your sessions to get the most results from the least amount of time? How do you put to use, or even simply learn, all of the information that's out there?

Most guitarists accumulate a big stack of magazine articles, instructional books, DVDs and videos throughout their years of playing. You might get overwhelmed when you consider how much information you have tucked away, never quite finding the time to absorb it all. Not to mention, if you can't find the time to absorb these ideas, how can you even begin to understand them and put them to good use in your playing?

Most people have "real" lives outside of music: jobs, school, bills, family, friends, etc. How can you meet your responsibilities, have a social life and still manage to squeeze in some practice time every now and then? Much of it comes down to priorities. Learn to recognize what is most important at any given time and what your daily commitments are. Then, think about what your goals are as a guitarist and what sacrifices you are willing to make to accomplish them.

No matter what you set out to achieve, whether it's becoming a better musician or getting a promotion at work, it boils down to two questions: "What do I want?" and "How hard am I willing to work to get there?"

When it comes to studying the guitar, learn to budget your time. Don't waste practice time *jamming* when you should be *practicing*. Jamming means playing what you already know and can literally play in your sleep. This is the kind of playing we do to entertain ourselves. Practicing means developing new skills and working them into your arsenal until you can use them at will, whenever, wherever and however you wish. At this point, exercises that were once challenging become part of your jamming repertoire, and you'll need to find new, more challenging exercises for practicing.

Going over the same bits that you can already play isn't progressing forward. If you're learning a new piece and can already play the first few pages easily, why keep going over them to get to the part where you get stuck? You should *isolate the difficult parts* and work on them until they become as easy to you as the earlier parts. Then, go back and play the whole thing.

It's a little like going to a buffet. Don't try to heap everything onto your plate at once. You can't enjoy all the different flavors lumped together anyway. But if you take a little at a time, you can really take the time to savor each item.

SOME TIPS FOR ORGANIZING YOUR PRACTICE TIME

- First of all, try to find a place and time for practice as free from distractions as possible.

- Now, let's say for the sake of argument that you have one hour set aside for practice time today. Let's divide this hour up and pick four areas in which you need to improve. For example:

    1. Alternate picking

    2. Legato techniques (hammer-ons and pull-offs)

    3. New chord voicings

    4. Arpeggios

- You now have four areas to work on and 60 minutes to practice. Take a few minutes at the start of the session to properly warm up. Then, divide the remaining time into four sections, each lasting about 10–15 minutes.

- If you can stick to this routine for just four days, with four one-hour sessions divided into four areas of study, you will progress at a much more well-rounded pace than if you had spent a solid hour on each topic. Even if you can only budget 30 minutes for a daily practice routine, if you budget your time in this manner, you'll be happy with your development of new and useful skills. Staying well-rounded and focused with a clear set of goals for yourself is paramount to growth. You don't want to focus on only one thing and leave others areas neglected.

- Here's another practice pointer: Wash your hands before you start to practice. This is a great ritual to work into your routine for a couple of reasons. First, it will get you into the right frame of mind. It will clear your mind of distractions so that you can concentrate on the task at hand: *practice*. It will also help warm up the muscles in your hands (especially on cold days or in cold venues before a performance) and will help promote flexibility and good blood flow. (The warmer the better in regards to water temperature.) Finally, clean hands help your strings last longer, and we all know that saving a couple of bucks is a good thing!

- Remember that in the end, it's still called *playing* music, not *working* music. It should always be fun. When something isn't fun, we tend to not want to continue; it's just human nature. *Never take the fun out of playing the guitar!*

- If you find yourself going over and over the same things, stop. Take a break. Don't sit there spinning your wheels, because you're only beating yourself up and sucking the fun out of it. When you reach this point, either move on or find something else to do. You don't want to burn yourself out. Keep it fresh, and it will stay fun.

THE ART OF PRODUCTIVE PRACTICE

Now that we've discussed how to budget your practice time and get into the right frame of mind, here are a few suggestions to help "tweak" or fine tune your practice sessions.

- **Always make sure your instrument is in tune before you start to practice**. The more time you spend playing and practicing, the stronger the connection becomes between your ears, hands and mind. You don't want to become accustomed to playing out of tune, because it will affect your ability to properly hear parts and find correct positions on the neck.

- **Always warm up your hands properly**. Many guitarists simply don't take the time to warm up the muscles of their hands before practicing or performing. This is especially important when it comes to playing more complex parts or accelerated speeds. Several great players have shortened their careers by not preparing their hands before attempting to play their instruments "full out." I cannot stress enough how important this is. Once your hands are warmed-up, you'll be surprised at how quickly new things will fall under your fingers. You'll have to learn to listen to your own biomechanics. For some people, it'll only take 10–20 minutes, while for others, an hour may be required to fully warm up. During cold seasons it may take even longer. You may find it beneficial when entering a cold venue or rehearsal area to put your hands under a faucet of warm running water and stretch gently to promote better blood flow and to warm the muscles of the hands.

- **Invest in a metronome**. A *metronome* (a device that makes a clicking sound at the *tempo*, or speed, of your choice) can be your best friend or your worst enemy. Developing a keen sense of timing is vital for any musician. The metronome (or a drum machine, which serves the same purpose) is an excellent tool for this. Knowing and understanding how to divide the beat is a crucial skill that will better both your rhythm playing and your lead phrasing. You may also use a metronome to keep track of how fast you can play the examples in this book. If you find that you can play something at a fast tempo, but not in time with the metronome's click, then you've developed speed but you lack control. Speaking of developing speed…

- **It is essential that you stay relaxed and loose**. Strive for small relaxed movements, and try to avoid flailing at the guitar. If you were asked to jump up and down as many times as possible in a 60-second period, would you leap for the ceiling each time, or would you take small skips like a boxer with a jump rope? The less wasted motion you have, and the closer the fingers of both hands stay to the strings, the quicker the transition time from string to string and position to position. This will allow you to play faster, cleaner and more efficiently. In other words, you'll be able to play faster with less effort.

- **Choke up on your pick!** Regardless of the gauge, shape or style of your chosen *plectrum* (a fancy word for pick), choking up on the pick and playing with the smallest portion of the tip will allow you the most control. There will be less pick sticking out, and that means less pick likely to become bogged down in the strings giving you resistance. Imagine your pick only just grazing the face of the strings. Now granted, there is a time and place to dig in and bash away at the strings with attitude, but for the advanced shredding techniques in this book, you'll find choking up on the pick to be more efficient.

- **Practice good muting.** *Muting* means silencing the strings that you aren't playing. This is crucial if you're using distortion at high volume. If you don't mute, you'll end up with a lot of feedback and/or string noise. You can mute the lower-pitched strings by lightly touching them with the palm of your picking hand or the inside of your forearm. You can mute the higher strings by lightly resting one or more fingers of your left hand against them. Good muting helps your playing sound smooth and relaxed.

While on the subject of staying relaxed during practice, let's consider the old sports adage: "Practice like you play." This means you should make the transition from rehearsal to the stage as uniform as possible by playing consistently in all situations. If your muscles are tense and tight when you practice, they become even more so under the stress of live performance. Once you add jitters and stage fright to the mix, your tight muscles will lock up and your playing won't be fluid. But, if you train those same muscles in a relaxed environment, they will be loose. When you get on stage and the adrenaline kicks in, your relaxed muscles will have room to adjust. You'll be able to get through the performance, and gradually, you'll find your groove and settle down.

Finally, if you find yourself mulling and stewing over a piece of music only to play up to the difficult part and then start all over again, STOP! Learn to isolate the difficult part and work only on that. You're wasting time going back and playing all the easy bits again and again. Woodshed on those difficult passages until they come just as easily, and then go back and work on putting all the pieces together. You'll be surprised at the speed of your progress and won't be nearly as stressed.

CHROMATIC CHAOS

The purpose of this section is to completely and thoroughly exhaust every finger combination we can come up with. (It's not possible to fit them *all* here, but this exercise will get you off to a pretty good start.)

The obvious question you may ask is, "Why?"

And the answer is this: The more absurd and demanding situations you put your fingers through in practice, the easier things become for you in real-world playing. What was once impossible will become possible.

The exercise below will develop great finger independence between the individual fingers of your fretting hand and will also synchronize the fretting and picking hands together. This will not happen overnight. It will demand dedication and patience. Using a metronome will greatly accelerate your progress.

Think of these examples as "jumbles" or "finger twisters." Most of them involve *chromaticism*. Chromaticism is movement up or down in *half steps* (the distance of one fret).

Up first is the "tried and true" method of chromatic fours. It's tried and true because it *works*. Try it using *alternate picking* (down-up, down-up) as shown and *legato* (using hammer-ons and pull-offs). Continue the exercise up an octave (12 frets) to the 13th *position* (1st finger on the 13th fret), and then start descending. (Many of the exercises in this book can be extended in this way.)

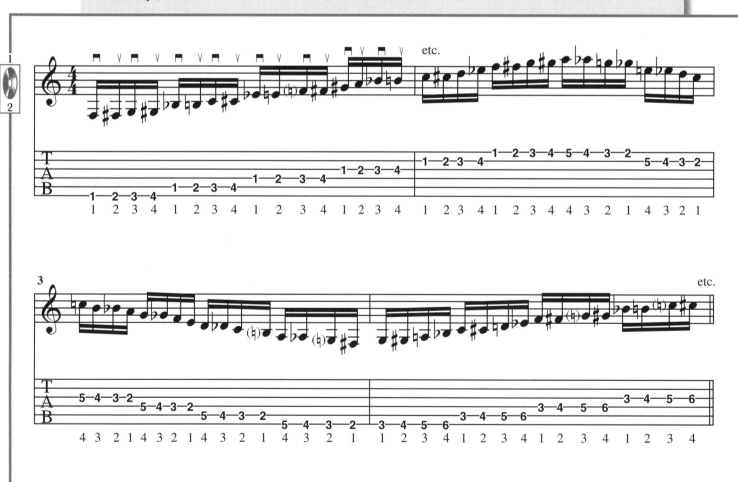

In Examples 2A and 2B, we'll use the fingerings 1–2–4 and 1–3–4. You will encounter these in the normal course of playing more often than the 1–2–3–4 fingering. If you're not accustomed to picking *triplets*, or groups of three notes in the time of two notes of the same value, take some time to get used to them before moving on. Most players have a little difficulty when picking across the strings in triplets. The tricky part is to strike the next adjacent string with an upstroke. Remember: patience and practice.

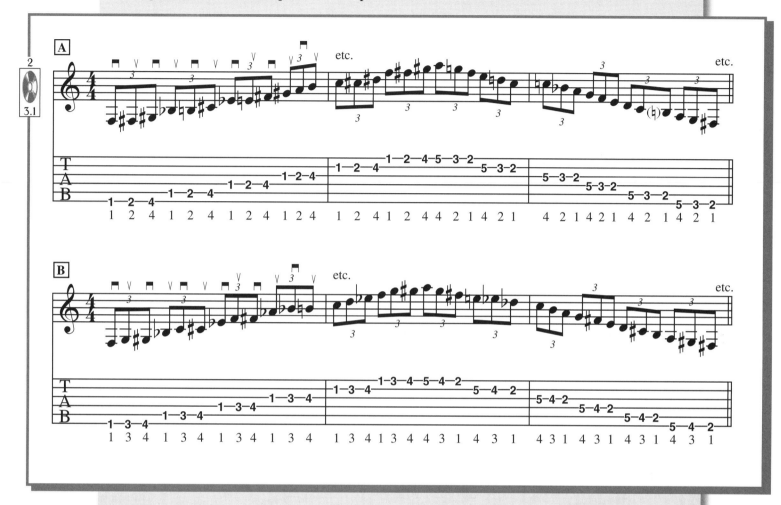

OUTSIDE PICKING

The finger twister that follows emphasizes a picking mechanic known as *outside picking*. This happens when the pick bounces or travels only on the outside faces of two strings. As a rule, most ascending picked passages that travel across the strings use outside picking.

INSIDE PICKING

The following example uses *inside picking*. This inside phenomenon happens when the pick bounces between two strings. Most people find this a little more difficult than outside picking, because it can feel like your pick is trapped between the strings. Try to stay as relaxed as possible, and it'll feel natural in no time.

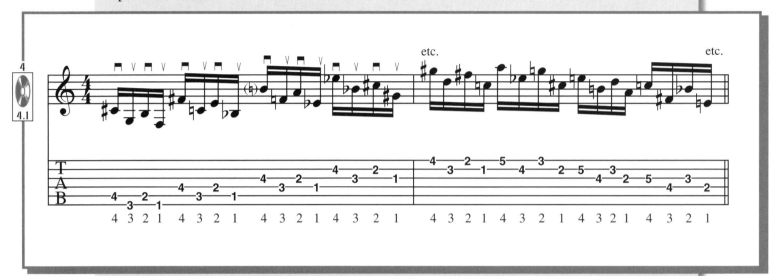

Examples 5A and 5B take us into four-note groupings played on adjacent strings with only one note per string. This, and the following one-note-per-string exercises, can come in handy both in your rhythm and lead playing—not to mention the improved accuracy and confidence you'll develop in your picking hand.

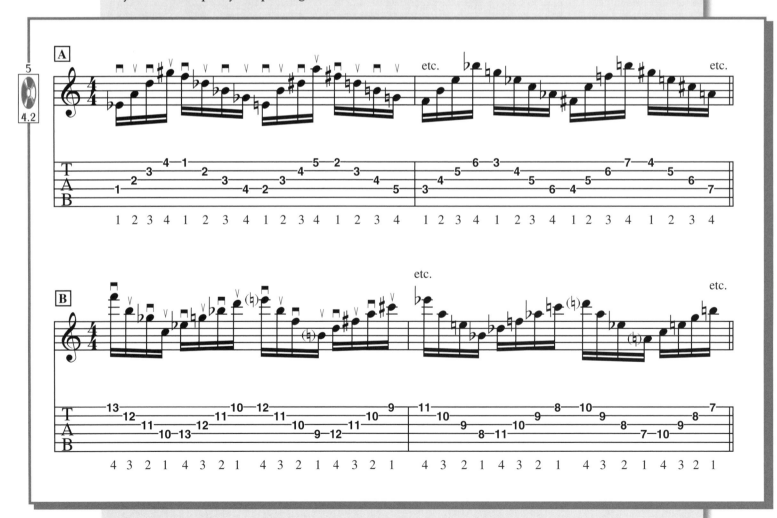

Examples 6A and 6B use triplet one-note-per-string patterns ascending and descending. You may notice that most of the exercises so far have a descending version that is the complete opposite (mirror image) of the ascending version. This is sometimes referred to as *retrograde motion*.

FINGER PERMUTATIONS

In Example 7A, we'll start every string with a different finger, cycling through all the possibilities: 1–2–3–4, 2–3–4–1, 3–4–1–2, 4–1–2–3.

In 7B, we'll do the same in reverse while descending: 4–3–2–1, 3–2–1–4, 2–1–4–3, 1–4–3–2. This is where these exercises truly become finger jumbles.

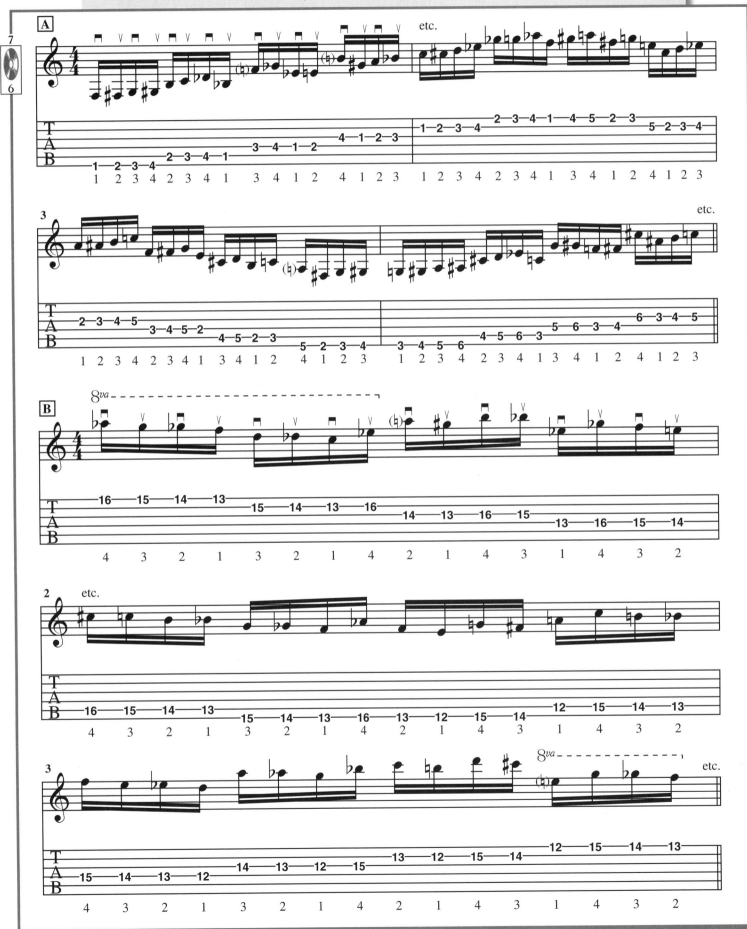

Example 8 will take you through these fingering combinations: 1–2–4, 2–4–1, 4–1–2.

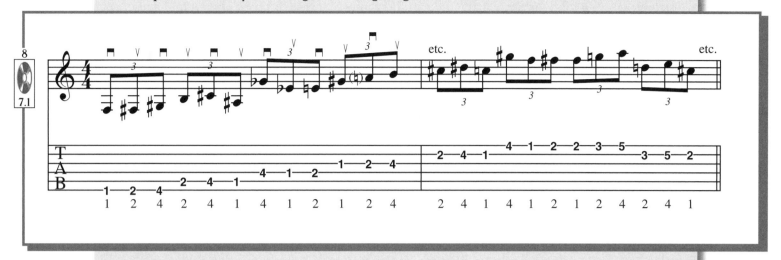

Example 9 uses these combinations: 4–2–1, 2–1–4, 1–4–2.

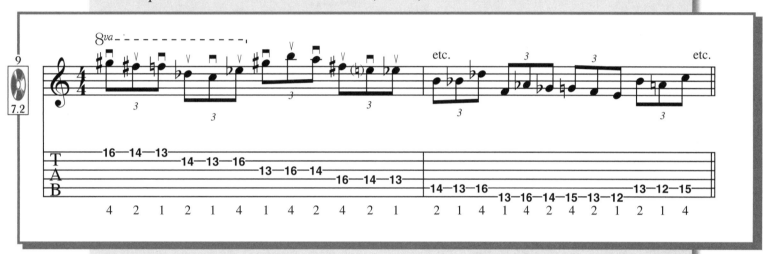

The rhythmic patterns in 10A and 10B are the same as in Examples 8 and 9, but the fingering is 1–3–4.

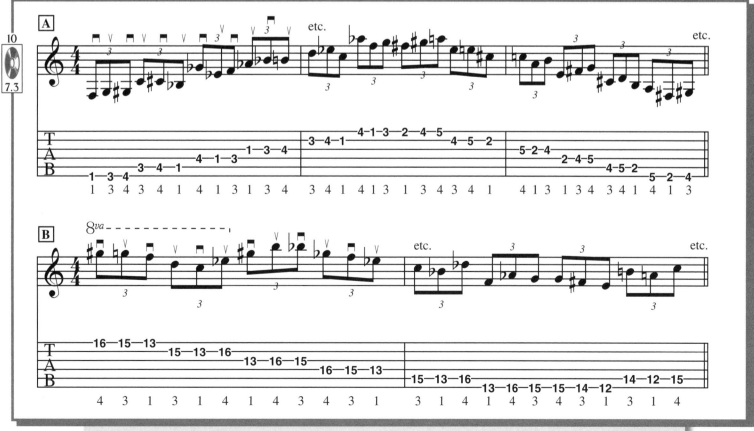

For Examples 11A and 11B, we'll use some unusual triplet groupings that fall across the strings in an angular fashion. Strive to keep the triplet feel even when using all four fingers to cross the strings.

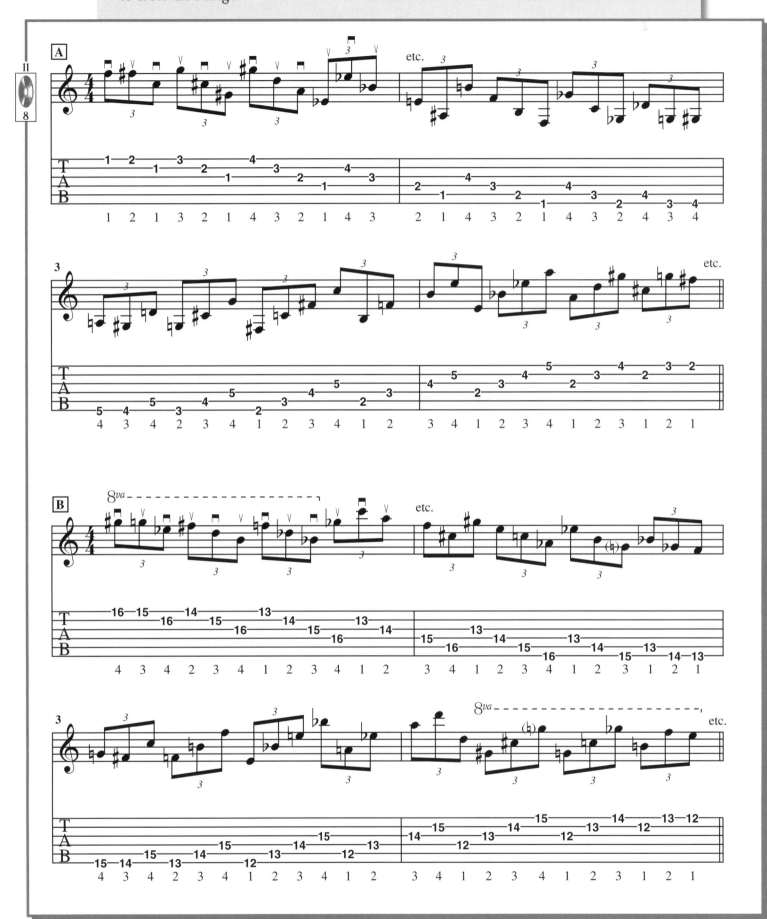

DOUBLE PICKING

Double picking is the order of the day in Example 12A and 12B. These rapid-fire four-note groupings can be used to create great solos and riffs. Double picking is when "groups" of four or more notes are broken down into miniature subdivisions of twos; usually it involves the doubling of individual notes in the style of Gary Moore, John Sykes and others.

PSYCHO TRIPLET EXERCISES

This brings us to the "Psycho Triplet Exercises." Examples 13A–13G are all really sick and twisted triplet patterns. Once you can manage these, you should be ready for just about anything anyone can challenge you with!

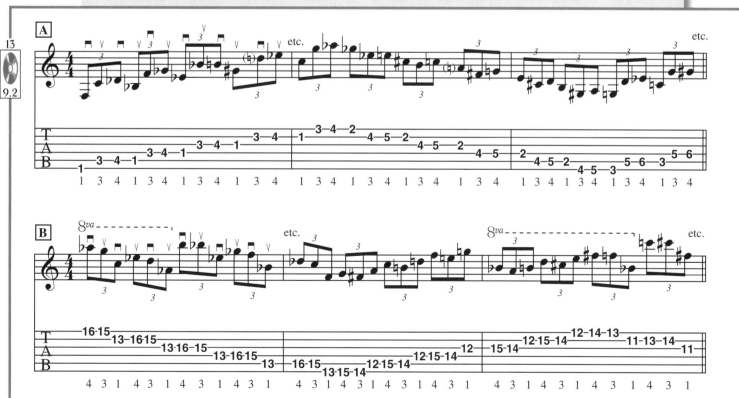

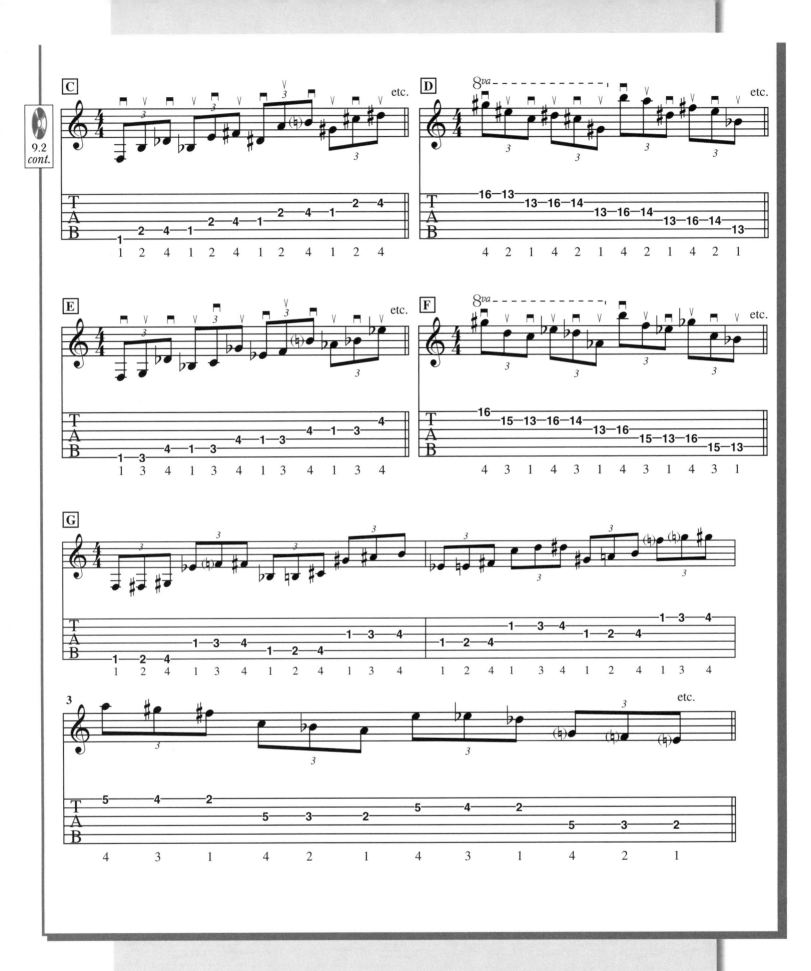

G BLUES LICK

For Example 14, we'll apply the inside picking technique to the *G Blues scale* in a descending flurry in the style of John Petrucci of Dream Theater and Liquid Tension Experiment. The G Blues scale is spelled 1–♭3–4–♭5–5–♭7 or G–B♭–C–D♭–D–F (see fretboard diagram below and also Major Scale Theory on page 21 for a quick review of scale degrees).

G Blues Scale

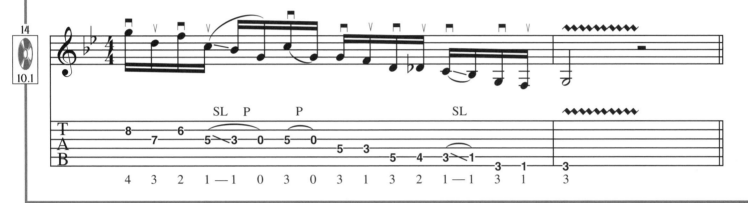

Note: The fingering above is only a suggestion. The example below shows an alternative in the context of a particular lick.

MORE PSYCHO TRIPLETS

Example 15 uses some of the displaced triplets (see note below) from the "Psycho Triplet Exercises" to ascend up the 1st and 2nd strings in the key of E Minor. We'll cap this one off with some classically-flavored *pedal tones*. Pedal tones are a melodic device where notes pivot around (rising or falling) a stationary note (or notes) called a pedal.

Note: The *displacement* in the three-note groupings is in how they are broken up on two strings as opposed to the more common triplet grouping of three notes ascending or descending on one string. This can cause accents and pick strokes to fall in unusual places giving a slightly "off-kilter" or displaced rhythmic inflection to both the player and the listener.

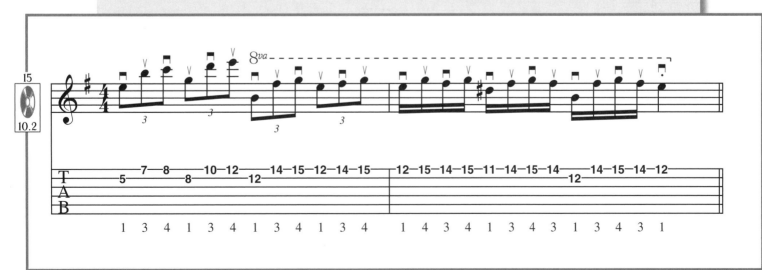

In Example 16, you'll find our outside picking technique mixed with some open strings in a B Minor ascending run. Note that you'll be starting these on an upstroke and bending a tapped high E (see page 61 for more on *tapping*).

Many guitarists choose to tap with their right-hand 2nd finger (*m*). The advantage to using the 2nd finger instead of the 1st is that you can tap while holding a pick. This adds fluidity to your playing and allows you to spontaneously add a tapped note to a picked pattern.

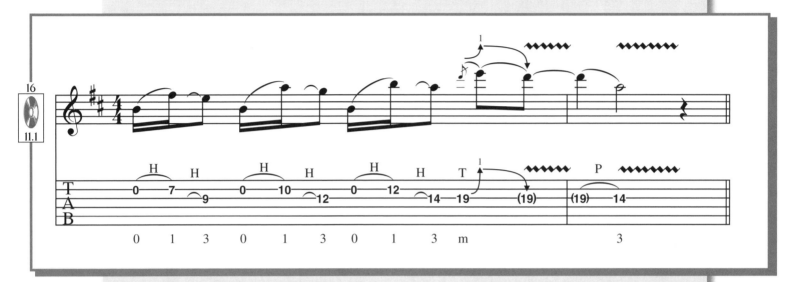

Example 17 is a *sextuplet* (sixteenth-note triplet) E Minor Pentatonic assault made up of groupings that ascend within themselves while actually descending the scale pattern. The CD contains recordings of this example at both slow and fast speeds. Many of the examples throughout this book are recorded at two speeds like this.

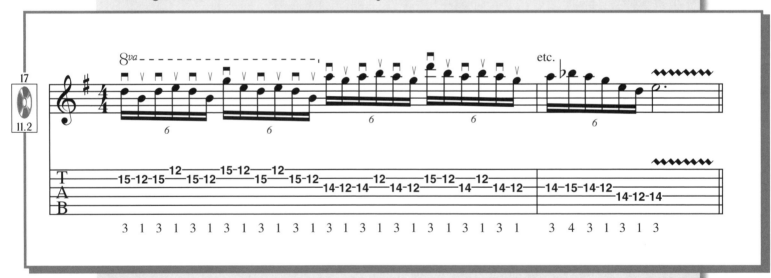

MORE DOUBLE PICKING

In this example, you'll use your double picking chops to outline a chord progression in E Minor. This type of rhythm playing can be heard in the playing of John Sykes (Whitesnake, Blue Murder, Thin Lizzy), Gary Moore, Michael Romeo (Symphony X) and many guitarists in the power metal genre as well. It's a great way to supplement a chord progression. It's also a cool alternative to tired-sounding power-chord chugging. Notice the use of *palm muting* (see page 95).

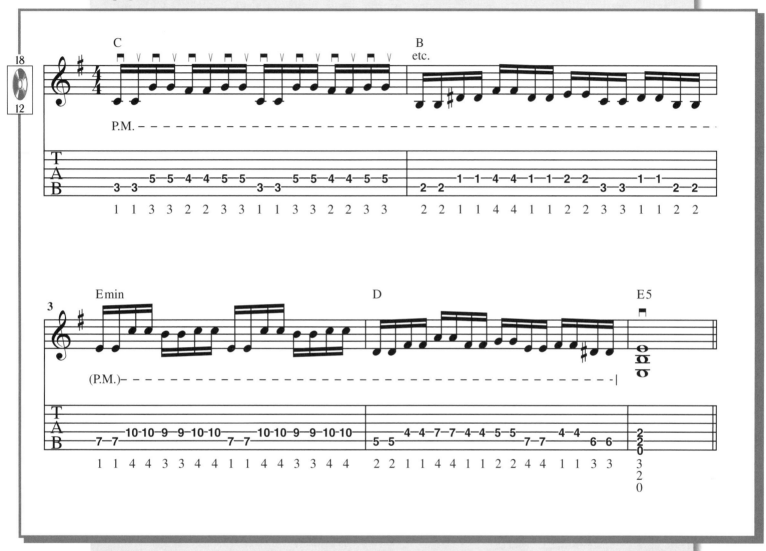

Major Scale Theory

Before moving on, let's take a moment to review the *major scale*. This scale has seven pitches, also known as *scale tones* or *scale degrees*, numbered 1–2–3–4–5–6–7. The first scale degree, from which the scale gets its name, is the *tonic*. All major scales have the same formula of *whole steps* (two frets) and *half steps* (one fret): Whole–whole–half–whole–whole–whole–half.

The Major Scale

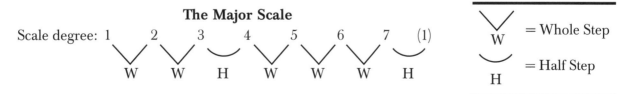

All other scales can be defined by using the degrees of the major scale as the standard. For example, if there is a half step between 2 and 3, instead of a whole step, we would call scale degree 3 a "♭3."

STRING-SKIPPING PEDAL TONES

Finally, for your review of this section, here is a string-skipping pedal-tone exercise in E Major. The E Major scale is spelled: E–F♯–G♯–A–B–C♯–D♯.

Master guitarists such as Al Di Meola and Eric Johnson have used small etudes like these to advance their string skipping and accuracy. These types of exercises also help to relax the wrist. *String skipping* is a technique used by modern soloists to create huge interval jumps without having to make large or abrupt shifts in fretting hand position. The end result is the illusion of sounding like the player has leapt from one end of the neck to another (and possibly back again) in the blink of an eye.

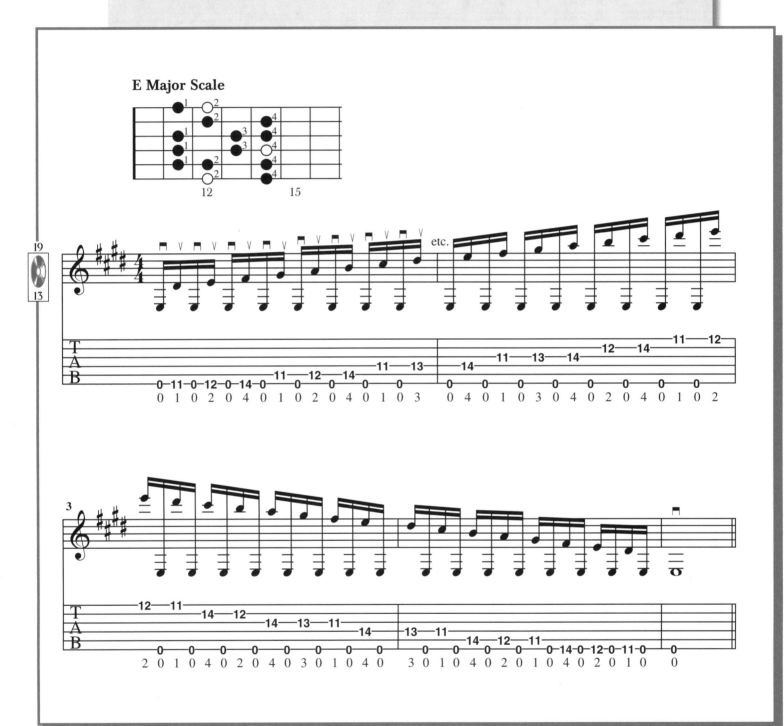

THE MODAL SYSTEM

The *modes* are a group of seven-note scales derived from the major scale (or its relative minor). The modes use the exact same notes as their "parent" major or minor scale, but with different starting and stopping points. Each mode has its own pattern of half steps and whole steps and therefore a new "flavor" or "color."

Here's an example of the progression of modes in A Minor. Most diehard rock and shred guitarists usually relate to minor keys more easily than major keys, because they are "heavier" or darker and more theatrical. A Minor is the parent scale/key. The natural minor scale is also known as the *Aeolian mode.* A Aeolian is spelled A–B–C–D–E–F–G.

Now, let's change the starting point to create a new mode. For example, the next mode is B *Locrian,* which is spelled B–C–D–E–F–G–A.

Here's the progression of modes in minor keys using A Minor as the parent scale/mode:

A Aeolian (natural minor)	A–B–C–D–E–F–G
B Locrian	B–C–D–E–F–G–A
C Ionian (major)	C–D–E–F–G–A–B
D Dorian	D–E–F–G–A–B–C
E Phrygian	E–F–G–A–B–C–D
F Lydian	F–G–A–B–C–D–E
G Mixolydian	G–A–B–C–D–E–F

The progression of modes in a major key would be as follows:

C Ionian (major)	C–D–E–F–G–A–B
D Dorian	D–E–F–G–A–B–C
E Phrygian	E–F–G–A–B–C–D
F Lydian	F–G–A–B–C–D–E
G Mixolydian	G–A–B–C–D–E–F
A Aeolian (natural minor)	A–B–C–D–E–F–G
B Locrian	B–C–D–E–F–G–A

We used C Major because it's the relative major key to the A Minor example at the top of the page.

SHAPE SHIFTING

Shape shifting is the practice of navigating up and down the fretboard using symmetrical melodic shapes and patterns found inside stock patterns for modes and scales. Shape shifting allows us to jump octaves and break the cycle of playing scales note-by-note.

A AEOLIAN MODE

Below, we have a 5th position fingering pattern for the A *Aeolian* mode (A–B–C–D–E–F–G). The formula for this mode is 1–2–$\flat3$–4–5–$\flat6$–$\flat7$ or W–H–W–W–H–W–W (W = whole step, H = half step).

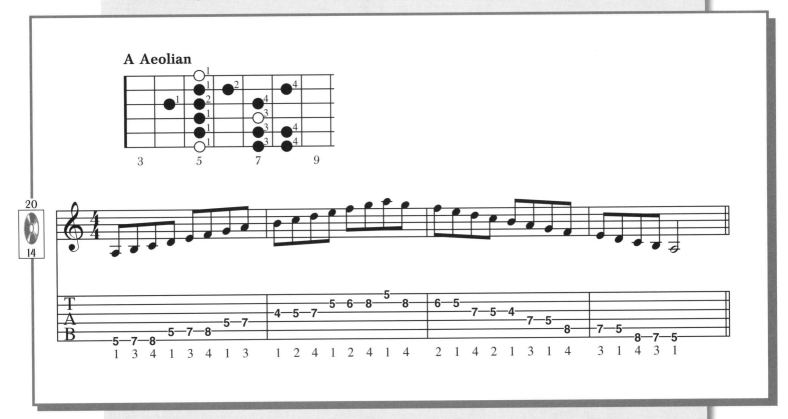

Most of the concepts and ideas presented in this book will be illustrated in the key of A Minor unless otherwise notated. A Minor is a great key for teaching new ideas for a couple of reasons: 1) If you are reading standard music notation (as opposed to TAB), there are no sharps or flats in most of the examples. 2) Regardless of the scale length or number of frets on your guitar's neck, A Minor usually sits nicely in the middle of the fretboard and you can easily play above and below. However, once you've gotten the hang of a new lick in A Minor, you should then go back and learn it in all of the other keys as well.

Example 21 (top of next page) illustrates the essence of many *Intelli-Shred* concepts. If we look at the first six notes of the A Minor pattern, we see that we have a repeating shape. Now, we'll shift this shape from the 5th position on the 6th and 5th strings, up to the 7th position of the 4th and 3rd strings (skipping the 7th note in the scale, G) where we find it repeats and then continuing on to the 10th position of the 2nd and 1st strings, where it repeats yet again. By simply omitting the G, you'll notice that we've broken out of the confines of the typical "box" pattern. Also, notice how easy it is to obtain a smooth, liquid run due to the fact that the fingering simply repeats for three octaves.

A Natural Minor (Aeolian)—Extended Pattern

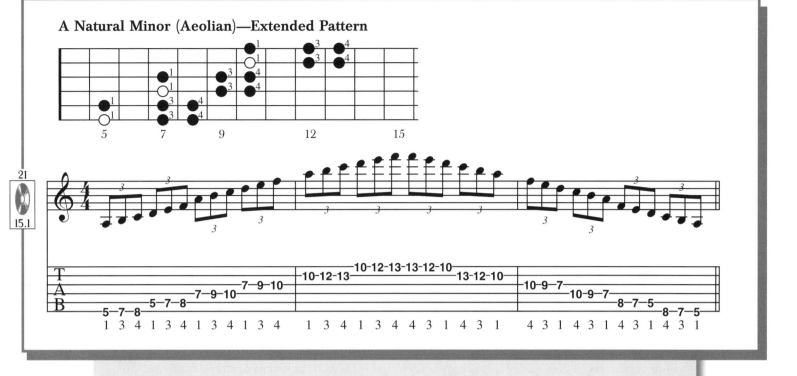

ARPEGGIOS AND FRETBOARD VISUALIZATION

Next, we have an A Minor triad shape (spelled A–C–E or 1–♭3–5). A *triad* is a type of three-note chord. This particular triad is an A Minor *arpeggio*. An arpeggio is the notes of any given chord played one at a time, as opposed to being strummed together. Notice while fingering this pattern that it resembles a triangle (see diagram below). You are practicing an important skill called *fretboard visualization*. There's a lot of geometry to the guitar's fretboard, and you will discover many triangles of various shapes and sizes. These minor triads often have a classical sound and have been used by players such as Uli Jon Roth, Ritchie Blackmore, Al Di Meola, the late Randy Rhoads and Yngwie Malmsteen. Here, we'll slide up to the high A to top it off.

A Minor Arpeggios

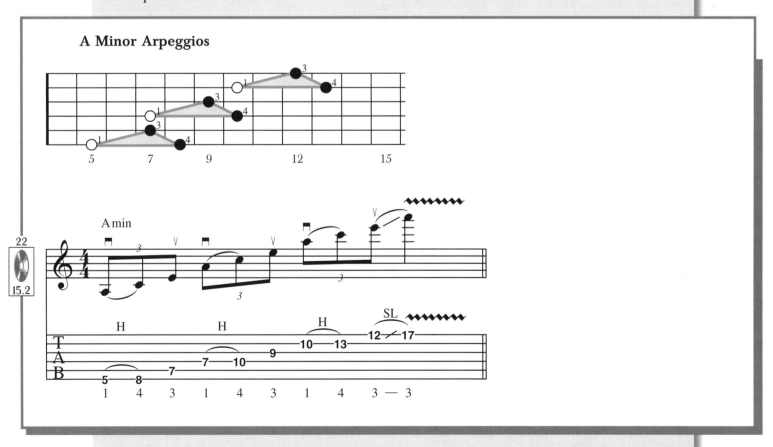

In Example 23, we'll use the same pattern, but with a sixteenth-note grouping and a finger-tapped high A note. An outside picking pattern consisting of a downstroke, hammer-on, then upstroke works well on this one. Just remember that *nothing* is carved in stone as an absolute. The phrasing marks shown on any of the examples are merely suggestions. Experiment and find what works best for you.

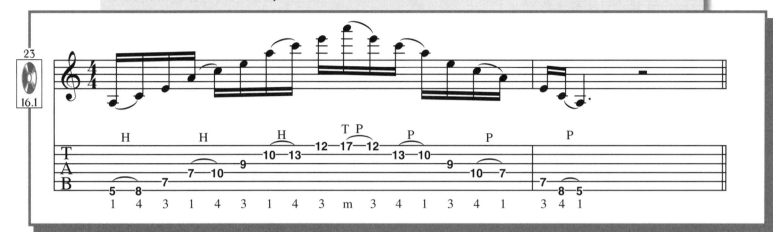

In the following example, the shape of the pattern is different (an inverted triangle), but the sequence of notes is the same: A–C–E. "Why use this pattern instead of the previous one?" you might ask. Look no further than Example 24. The stretches are a little wider, but this particular rhythm and phrasing would've been clunky and awkward using the previous pattern. Watch out for the *staccato* (short, detached) notes in 24B. They are indicated by the dots above or below the noteheads.

A Minor Arpeggios

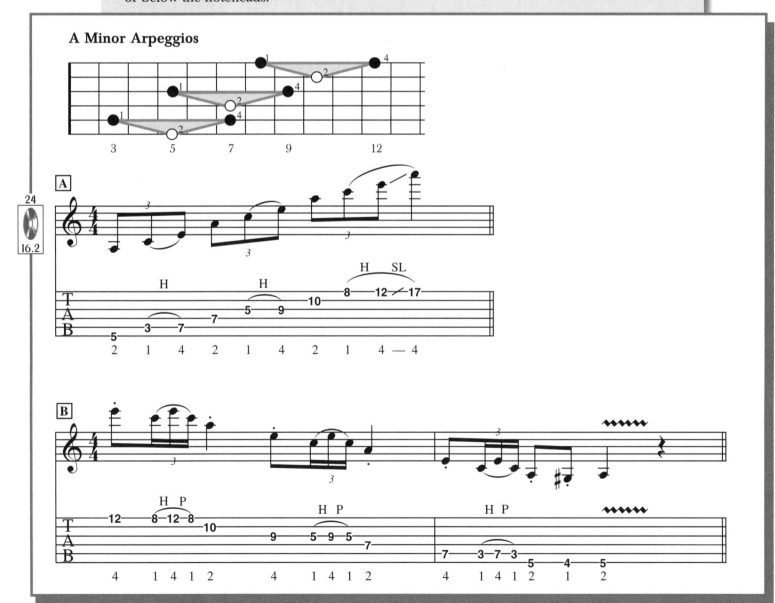

In the following example, we're going to transform this outline into a *minor 7th chord*. This particular pattern is for the Amin7 chord (A–C–E–G). Here, it will be spelled out G–A–C–E or $^b7$–1–$^b3$–5. This grouping, or *inversion*, allows for a nice sixteenth-note run taking us through the 3rd, 5th and 8th positions. (An inversion is a chord voicing that does not have the root as its lowest note.)

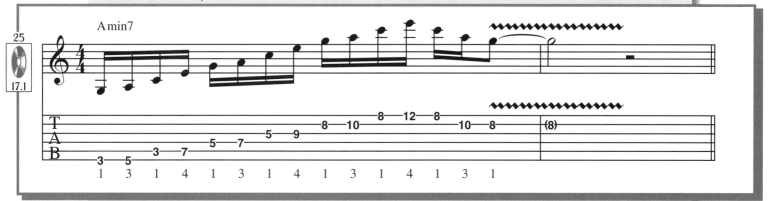

B LOCRIAN MODE

The next mode in the series is B *Locrian* (B–C–D–E–F–G–A). Locrian is sometimes called "the lost mode" for its unfinished, unresolved sound. This is due to our ears expecting a resolution to a major or minor "one" chord. The Locrian sounds "diminished" (though it is not a true diminished scale; see page 51) or "exotic" due to the $^b2$ and $^b5$. It is spelled 1–$^b2$–$^b3$–4–$^b5$–$^b6$–$^b7$ or H–W–W–H–W–W–W. The Locrian mode can be used over a diminished 7th or min7$^b5$ chord. Many metal riffs have taken advantage of its sinister side in highlighting the $^b2$ and $^b5$. You'll also notice that this mode, despite its new "box," is simply a re-spelling of A Aeolian now starting on the 2nd note.

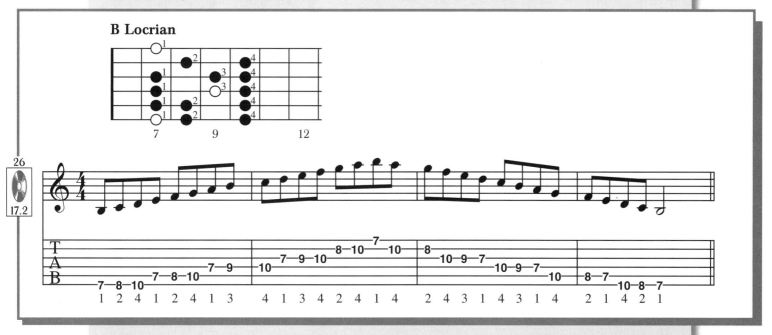

As in the previous Aeolian examples, we'll drop the 7th note (A) and use a repeating six-note pattern (B–C–D–E–F–G). Anytime the patterns match like this on adjacent strings, we can take advantage of that fact to make smooth, extended runs up and down the neck.

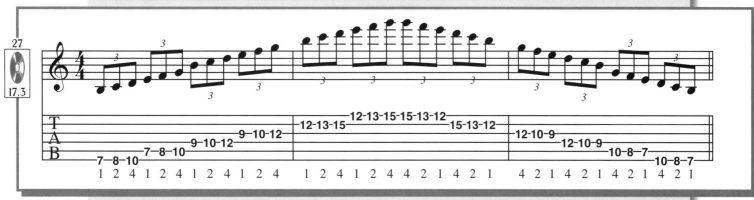

Example 28 starts with the first octave-jumping pattern we did in A Minor (Example 21, page 25), ascending to B Locrian, and finally descending to make one big looping lick. You'll hear "musical U-turns" like this one in the playing of Paul Gilbert and others.

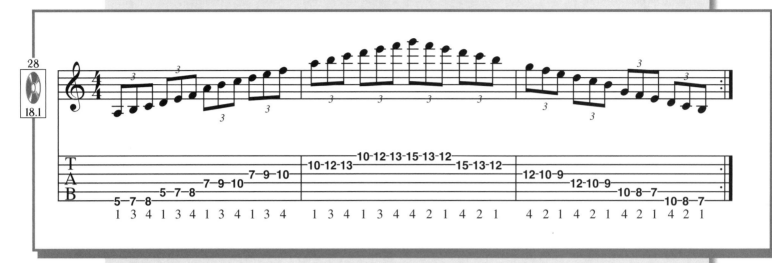

Next up is a cool little sequence outlining a CMaj7 chord (spelled B–C–E–G or 7–1–3–5). The ending features some jazzy finger slides and a chromatic descending line in the last octave to add to the fusion flavor.

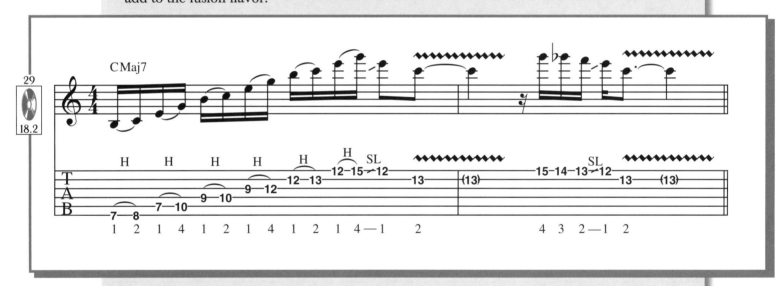

Example 30 takes advantage of the Locrian mode's diminished flavor to serve up a little neo-classical "doom and gloom." It then resolves back to A Minor.

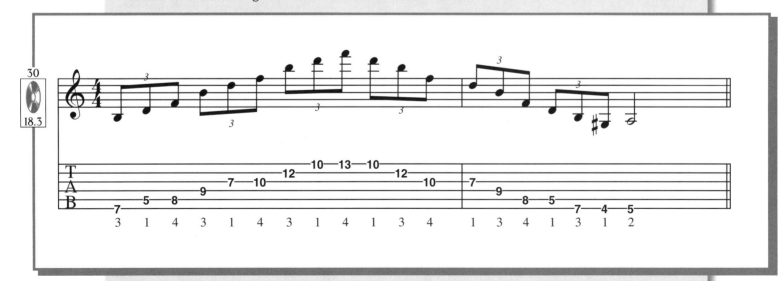

The following example has even more of a "classical" sound due to the phrasing. You'll notice an ascending A Minor triad in a four-note grouping moving up to a B Diminished shape and then descending to a G♯ Diminished pattern. Notice the triangle shapes again.

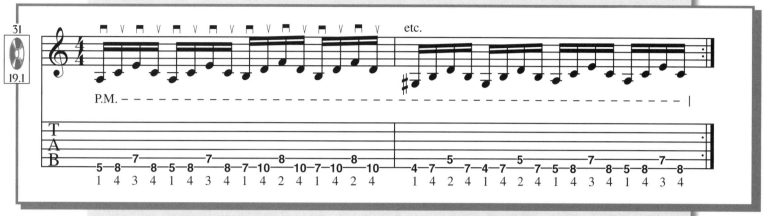

C IONIAN MODE

This brings us to the C *Ionian* mode, otherwise known as the major scale. Anyone who has ever been around a beginning piano student will recognize its sound. The C Major scale is spelled C–D–E–F–G–A–B or 1–2–3–4–5–6–7.

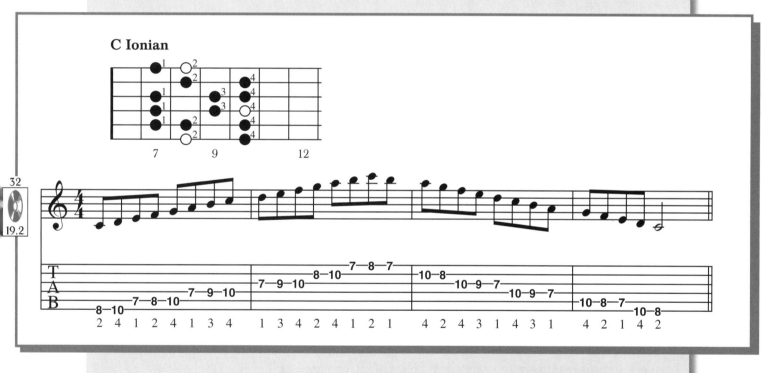

Below, we've taken the notes C–E–G and spelled out a C Major triad. Again, take note of its triangular shape as it moves through three octaves. Feel free to experiment with tapping the high C note as opposed to sliding into it. Using triad patterns like this is a great way to outline an underlying chord progression as part of a solo, melody or riff.

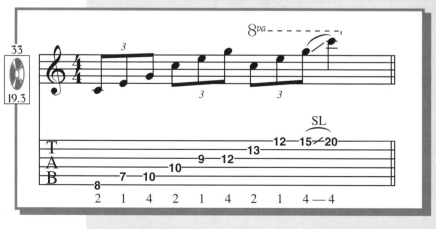

Example 34 takes the first six notes of C Ionian and rearranges them into three-note-per-string groupings.

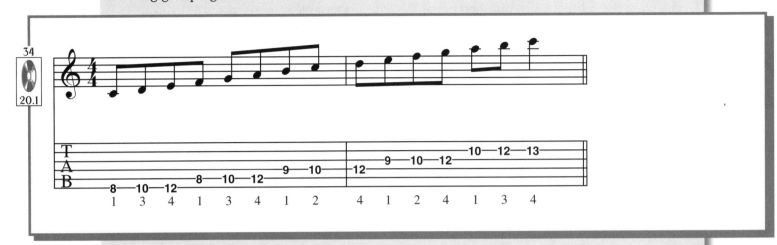

This next example doubles some of the string lines to make sextuplet phrases that are suited for both legato and alternate picking. Try both. You'll see that using hammer-ons and pull-offs produces a smooth sound, and the alternate picking version will have that "machine gun" staccato or aggressive tone.

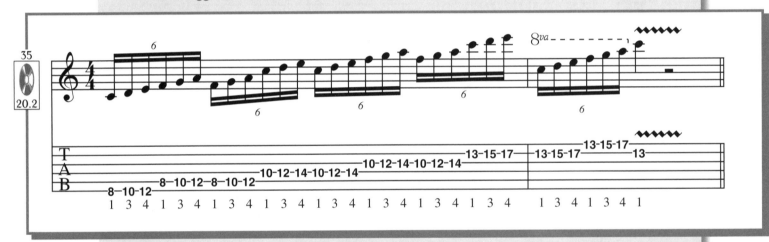

Example 36 makes use of some legato slides in the fretting hand to add a "slippery" quality to the phrasing. These legato slides can be heard in the style of players such as George Lynch. Don't let the odd note clusters (*septuplets*, or groups of seven) intimidate you. It's more important to *feel* them than to have them mathematically perfect. You don't want them to feel stiff. Just take your time working them up to speed. With a little patience, they'll eventually feel natural.

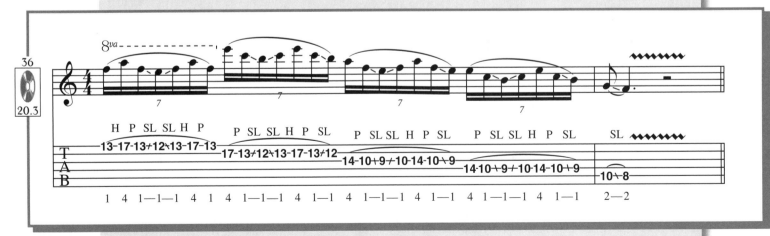

Once again, we have a pattern that highlights the tones of a C Major 7 chord. This particular pattern is interesting because it lacks the chord's root, C. It also includes the 4th, F, so that it fits into three-note-per-string groupings. If you have a tremolo arm (a.k.a. whammy bar) on your guitar, check out the *bar dips* (downward pitch bends) at the end.

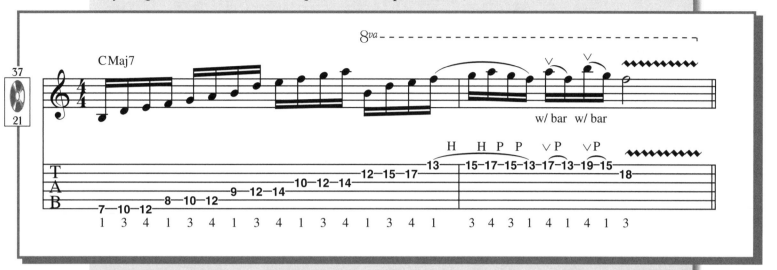

D DORIAN MODE

Next up is the *Dorian* mode. The Dorian mode isn't quite as dark or heavy as the Aeolian mode. It is spelled 1–2–♭3–4–5–6–♭7. It has a lighter tonality because it has a natural 6th instead of a flat 6th like Aeolian. Dorian is a great alternative in situations where the Aeolian mode feels a bit too gloomy. It sounds good over a minor 7 chord. It also mixes very nicely with minor pentatonic or minor blues-based lines.

You'll hear this mode in the playing of a lot of '70s rock and fusion players. For some great Dorian-based playing, take a listen to Carlos Santana or Tony Iommi of Black Sabbath.

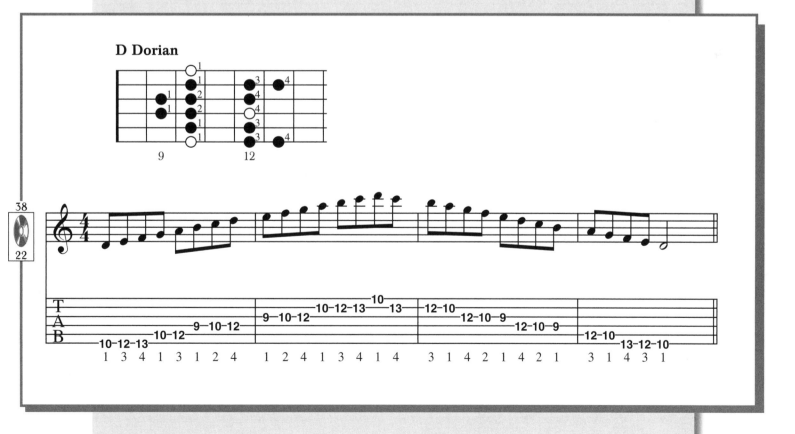

Example 39 uses the first six notes (D–E–F–G–A–B) arranged into three-note-per-string groupings. This creates three groups of two-string patterns and allows for easy octave jumping.

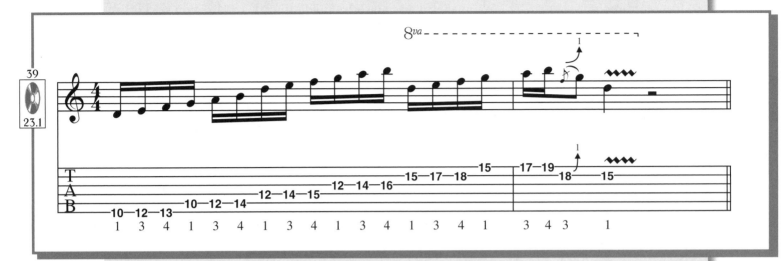

As mentioned previously, the Dorian mode sits nicely over a minor 7th chord. That's because all the notes of the minor 7th chord (1–♭3–5–♭7) are also contained in the Dorian mode (1–2–♭3–4–5–6–♭7). The shape used in the following example is the same as in Example 25 (page 27), which also featured a minor 7th chord. This pattern ascends three octaves and then descends using the D Blues scale. There's even a string skip thrown in for good measure.

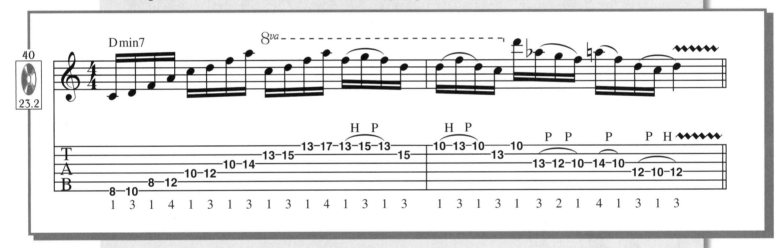

Now, we'll revisit our six-note grouping and get a little creative with the sequencing of the notes. Notice how changing the order of notes makes this line sound more interesting, as if it's going "against the grain" of the beats.

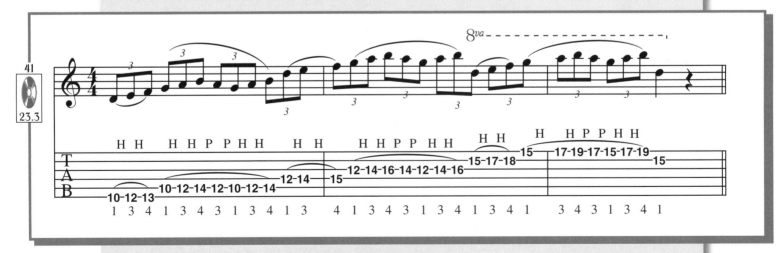

E PHRYGIAN MODE

The *Phrygian* mode is spelled 1–♭2–♭3–4–5–♭6–♭7. It is a long-time staple of Spanish and Middle Eastern music, as well as tons of rock and metal bands. The ♭2 lends to its evil or sinister sound. You'll hear this mode getting a good workout in the music of Al Di Meola, Deep Purple, Metallica, and many others.

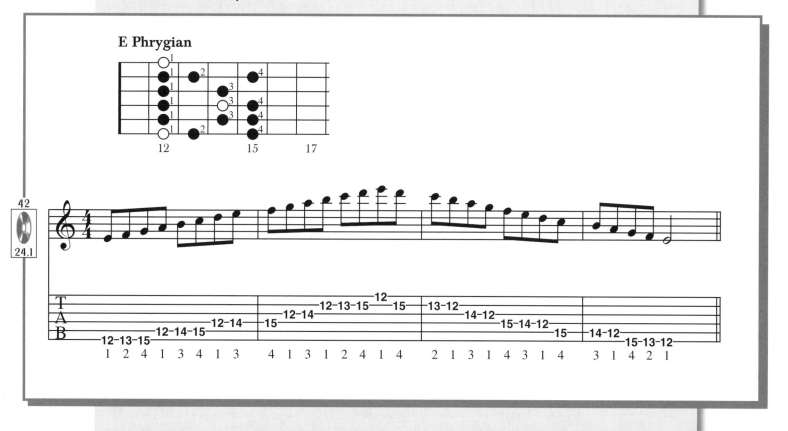

You should be familiar with the routine by now: We'll take the first six notes (E–F–G–A–B–C) and run them across the neck in an angular fashion for three octaves.

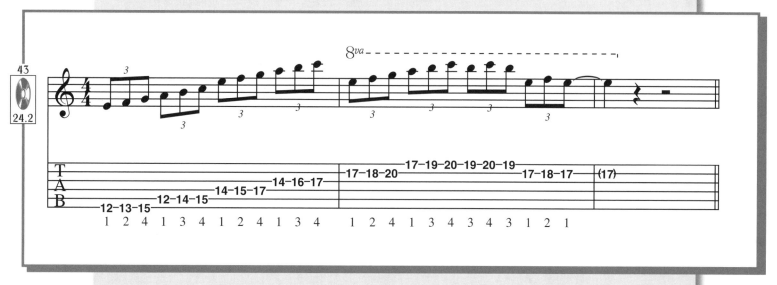

This time, we're going to omit a few more notes and use just 1–♭2–4–5 to make a haunting little passage.

We'll use whammy bar dips to attack the first note of each four-note group instead of picking. If you don't have a whammy bar, try sliding into the note instead. Also, there's a half-step bend-and-release that rises and falls from B up to C then back to B. The effect is to "tickle" the listener's ear, creating a comfortable resting place (usually the 1, 4 or 5) and then take it away again. This draws the listener's attention into the piece.

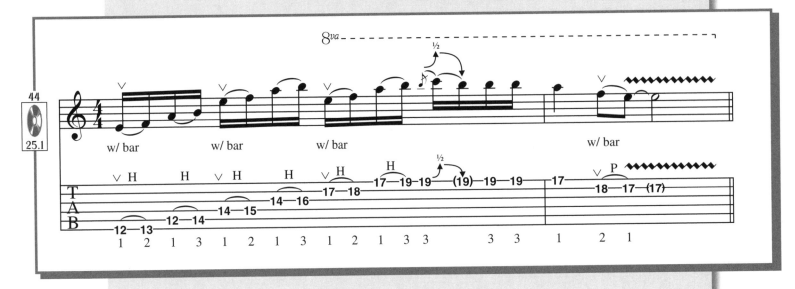

Here's a sixteenth-note descending legato passage using E Phrygian. You may find a tendency to rush these groupings, because they easily fall into a triplet or sextuplet feel. Keep them steady in groups of four. The last note is an *artificial harmonic* (see page 95).

F LYDIAN MODE

The *Lydian* mode is heard in the playing and writing of guitar giants such as Joe Satriani and Steve Vai. You'll also hear it in many movie soundtracks. It's known for its "dreamlike" quality. Lydian is basically the major scale with a raised 4th degree, spelled 1–2–3–♯4–5–6–7. F Lydian, the 6th mode of A Minor (A Aeolian) is F–G–A–B–C–D–E.

The Lydian mode sits nicely over the VI chord in a minor key progression or the IV chord in a major key progression. It is also the perfect mode to use over a major ♯11 chord.

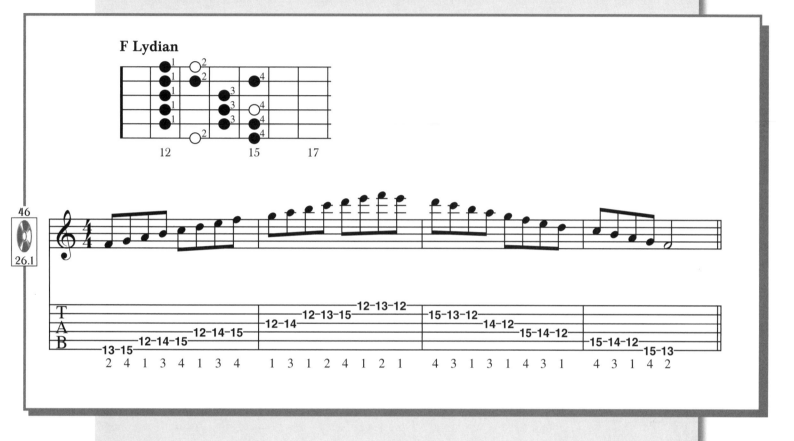

It may take a little while to wrap your brain around the Lydian sound, but once you do, you'll be able to do wondrous things. To really hear and feel this mode, try this exercise using the Lydian triad: 1–3–♯4, or F–A–B. Once again, use the tremolo bar to dip into and attack the indicated notes instead of using the pick.

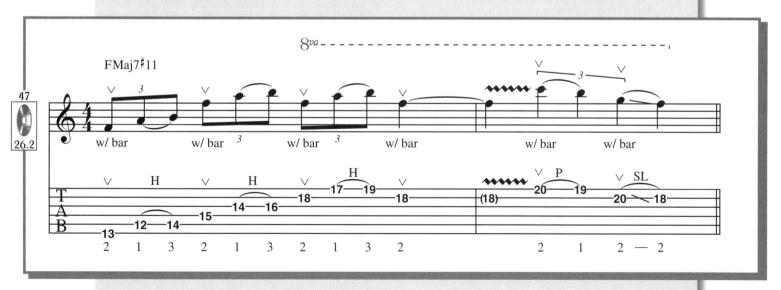

Example 48 uses a major triad with an added 2nd (1–2–3–5). This is a great "one size fits all" pattern to use over any chord with a major 3rd. Try this pattern over any of the following chord types: Maj, add9, add11, dominant 7, Maj7, etc.

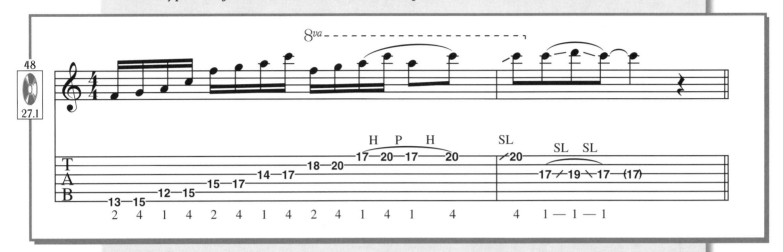

The following example uses big legato passages in the style of guitarists such as Allan Holdsworth or Joe Satriani. Be warned, however: There are some wide hand stretches here along with some big position shifts as you ascend, so please, be careful! Warm up carefully and practice slowly so you don't hurt your hands. Also, don't let the odd five-note groupings throw you off. Take the time to really feel them so they sound as fluid as possible.

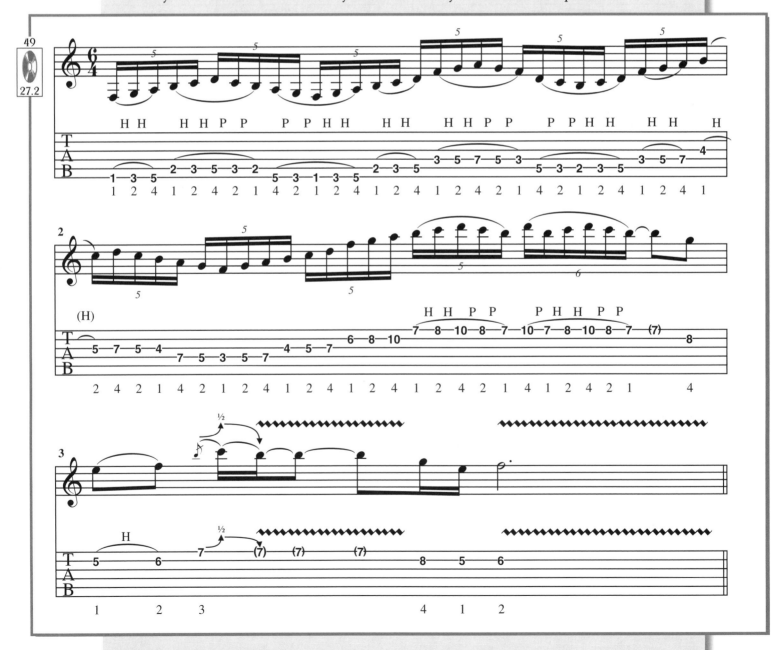

G MIXOLYDIAN MODE

The *Mixolydian* mode is a major scale with a flat 7th. It is spelled 1–2–3–4–5–6–♭7 or G–A–B–C–D–E–F. It sounds best over a dominant 7 chord and is found in a wide range of music, from blues to swing to jazz to rock. You'll hear the Mixolydian mode in the playing of Jeff Beck, Eddie Van Halen, Joe Satriani, Vernon Reid, Jimmy Page, Stevie Ray Vaughan, Eric Johnson and many others.

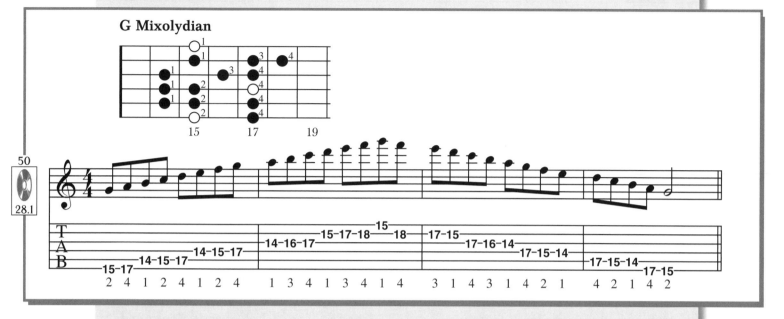

The following example is a real crowd-pleaser, good for cutting loose over an upbeat boogie or blues-based summertime rocker. For variety, try mixing in some major pentatonic and/or minor pentatonic licks.

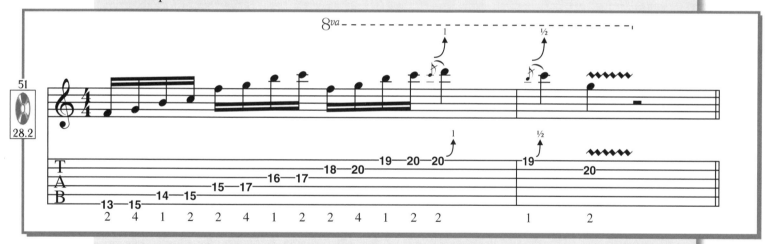

Example 52 features what can be best described as the Mixolydian triad (1–3–♭7). These three notes outline the sound of a dominant 7 chord. Bends are used to really bring out the bluesy goodness. Take your time with the bend at the end; bend slowly and really make it "sing."

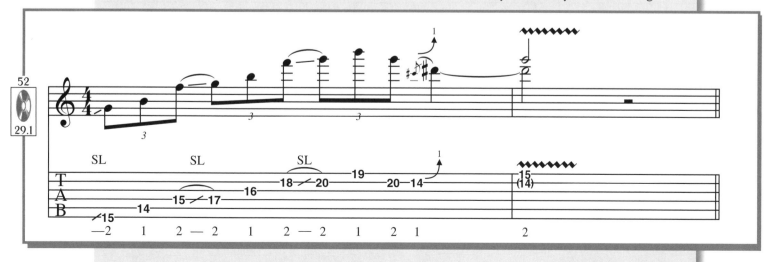

Here is a crazy, string-skipping G Mixolydian lick with legato shift slides. This is a slippery one!

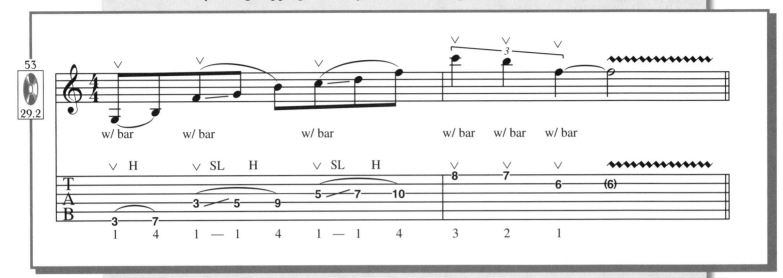

HARMONIC MINOR SCALE

The *harmonic minor scale* (1–2–♭3–4–5–♭6–7) is one of the most dramatic and theatrical of all the scales and modes. It is simply the Aeolian (or natural minor) scale with a natural 7th. However, this one changed note makes a huge difference in sound. While the natural minor scale and all of its modes are constructed entirely of half steps and whole steps, the harmonic minor scale contains a minor 3rd (a whole step plus a half step) between its 6th and 7th scale degrees. The A Harmonic Minor Scale is spelled: A–B–C–D–E–F–G♯.

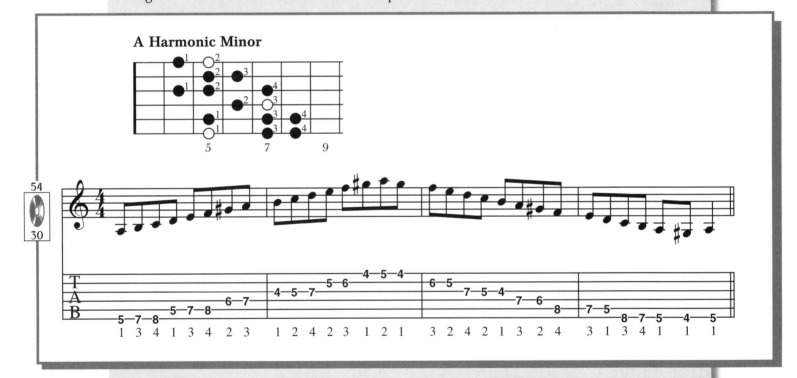

If you are seeking deep, dark and powerful six-string wizardry, Example 55 is for you. This example makes for a great angular run up the fretboard.

A HARMONIC MINOR SCALE LICK OF DOOM

Now here's another helping of neo-classical shred goodness in a descending line using six-note groupings. Try this one both as a legato line and with alternate picking.

PHRYGIAN ALTERED SCALE

Example 57 features the *Phrygian altered scale*, the sinister cousin of the harmonic minor scale. It is sometimes called the *Phrygian dominant scale* because it is the 5th mode of the harmonic minor scale. (You can create modes from any scale by starting it on different scale degrees, just as we did earlier with the natural minor scale.) The Phrygian altered scale is spelled 1–♭2–3–4–5–♭6–♭7 or E–F–G♯–A–B–C–D.

This scale instantly conjures up images of shifting sand, dungeons, dragons and evil wizards. No scale sounds more "metal" than this one!

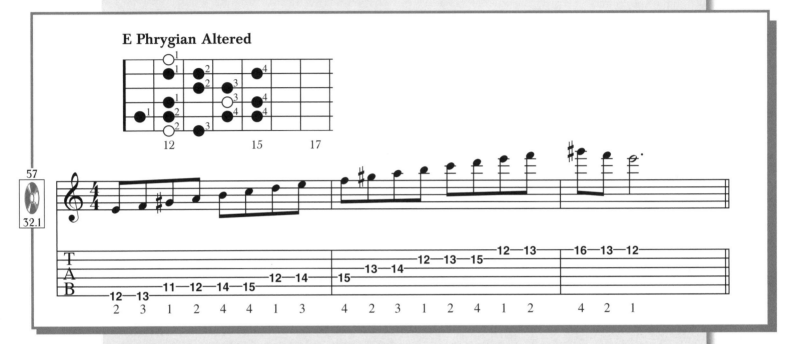

This is a snaky line consisting of five-note groupings. Let the third bar breathe and mind the quintuplet flurry on beat 4.

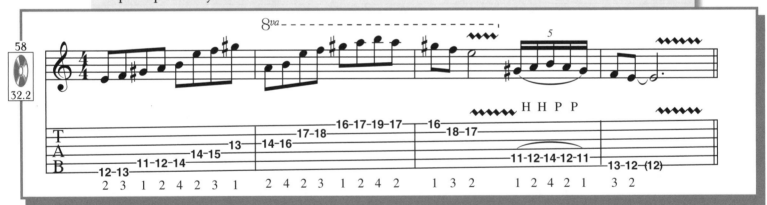

Example 59 applies our six-note, two-string grouping to the Phrygian altered scale, adding a jump to cover a full three octaves. You'll hear lines like this used by neo-classical players like Yngwie Malmsteen, Tony MacAlpine and Vinnie Moore. Once you're familiar with the unique sound of Phrygian altered, try to come up with your own ideas.

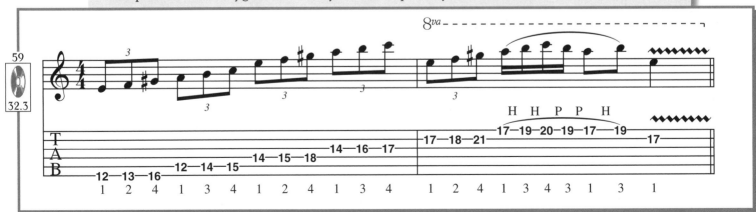

Here's another short lick featuring the Phrygian altered scale.

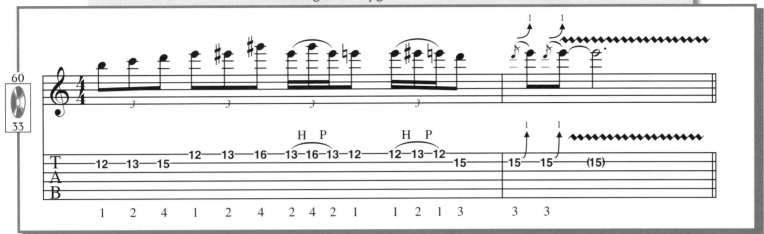

BLUES SCALE AND MINOR PENTATONIC EXTENSION

Example 61 is a review of our old friends the blues scale and the minor pentatonic extension. Make sure you are comfortable with these two scales before moving on.

In Examples 62A and 62B, we're going to start jumping octaves with the pentatonic scale. Most players find it difficult to run up and down the neck using this scale, limiting them to phrases in a fixed position. The next few examples will help liberate you from the same old fixed-position patterns. Pentatonic scales have the reputation of being rock clichés, but players such as Eric Johnson and Zakk Wylde know that pentatonic scales are just as good for jumping around the neck as any other scale.

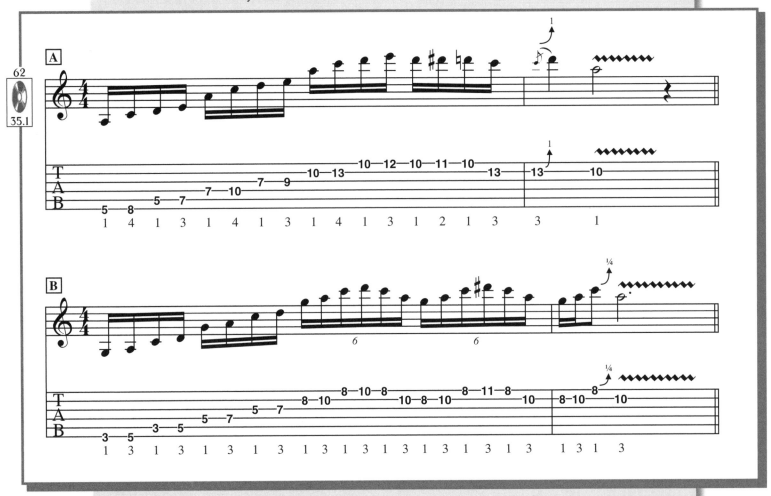

To add a little color to Example 63, try using a wah-wah pedal if you have one. Also, pay attention to the bluesy little bends and staccato notes. Don't rush these techniques; take your time and squeeze as much emotion from them as possible.

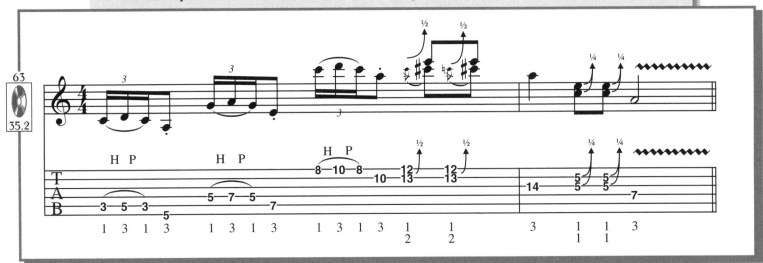

Here's a greasy legato line in the style of Paul Gilbert and George Lynch.

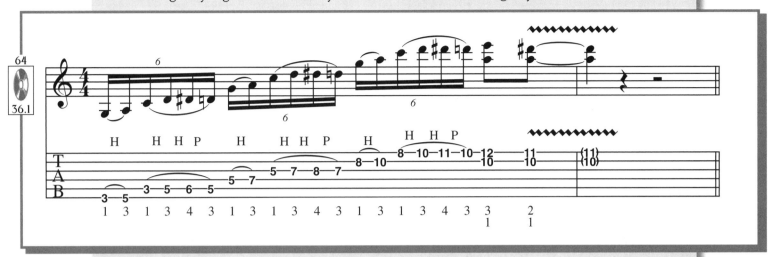

Here's a little more southern-fried, flat-five goodness. More gravy anyone?

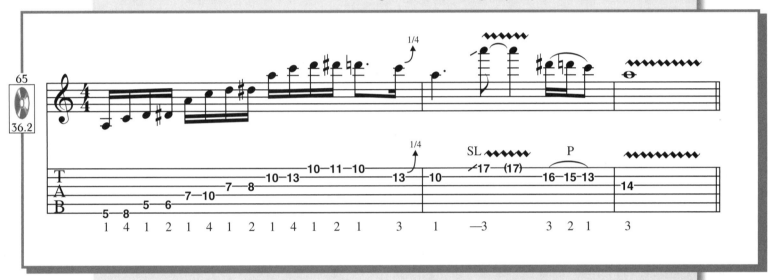

Example 66 uses the blues scale, adapted for six-note groupings. It is a familiar scale, but perhaps an unfamiliar fingering if you are used to playing it in the box pattern. Take some time to get acquainted with this pattern. Finding all of the E's in advance will help you through this one.

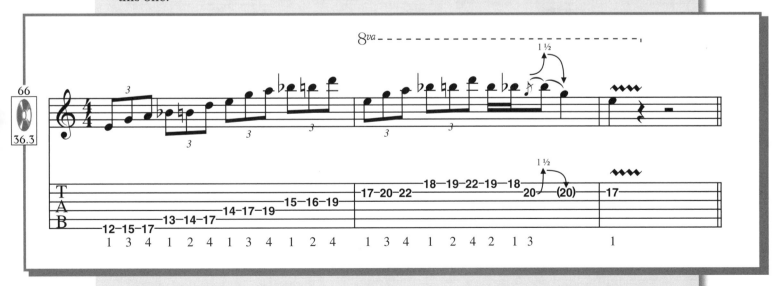

Following are some additional patterns and runs for your pentatonic pleasure.

MINOR 7TH ARPEGGIO PATTERNS

Here is a new pattern for outlining a minor 7th chord. This example uses notes from the Amin7 chord: 1–♭3–♭7 or A–C–G.

As you look closely at this pattern below, you'll see that the notes form yet another triangle pattern. You may find this one easiest to play using the 1st and 3rd fingers of the left hand.

Example 69 demonstrates how to transpose minor 7ths and minor triads across the i, iv and v chords of a minor key. The result is a series of minor 7th triads in the key of A Minor that ascend through the i–iv–v or Amin–Dmin–Emin progression. These use the triplet-triad triangle shape. The second guitar (Gtr. II) is playing the chords being outlined by the first guitar (Gtr. I).

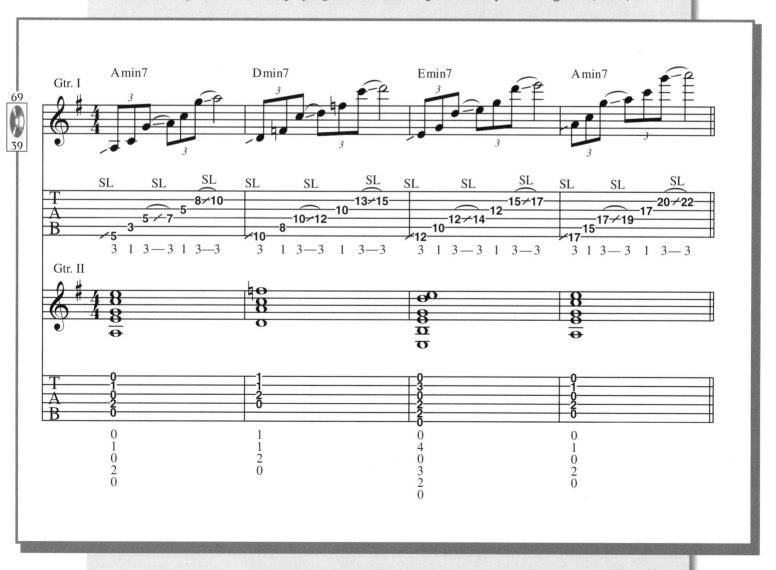

Now try transposing four-note groupings using sixteenth notes through the i, iv and v chords.

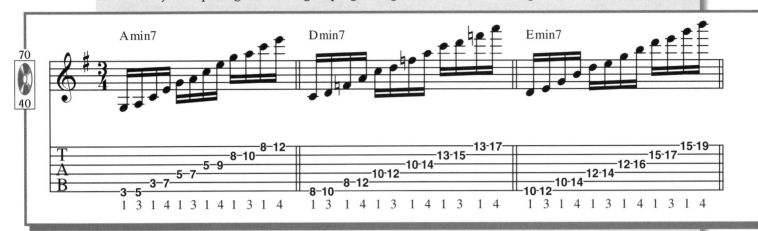

Think about this: The previous two examples worked because the i, iv and v modes in a minor key (Aeolian, Dorian and Phrygian) all contain the notes 1–♭3–♭7. We will delve deeper into minor key theory throughout this book.

EXTENDED ARPEGGIOS

The root, 3rd, 5th and 7th are considered the "standard" notes in any type of 7th chord or arpeggio. Sometimes, you'll see a chord symbol containing the numbers 9, 11 or 13. This indicates you should add one or more notes, called *extensions*, for a more "colorful" or "complex" sound. An *extended chord* can be built from a major 7th (Maj9, Maj11, Maj13), minor 7th (min9, min11, min13) or dominant 7th (9, 11, 13) chord. Extensions are cumulative, meaning an 11th chord may also contain the 9th, and a 13th chord may also contain the 9th and/or 11th. You may wonder where the numbers 9, 11 and 13 are coming from, since there are only seven notes in the scale. The answer is that they are simply the 2nd, 4th and 6th played one octave higher. Extended chords sound muddy if you try to play all the notes in the same octave, so moving the extensions up an octave spreads the chord out and gives each note room to "breathe." The voicings for extended chords can be complicated, but by breaking them up into arpeggios, it's easier to learn how they're constructed. Let's look at some examples.

Example 71A takes us through an arpeggio for an Amin11 chord. To build Amin11, start with Amin7 (1–♭3–5–♭7), then add the extensions (9–11) to spell 1–♭3–5–♭7–9–11 or A–C–E–G–B–D. The voicing used for the arpeggio in this example covers a wide range of over 2 octaves.

You can create many possible voicings for extended arpeggios by moving notes up or down an octave, or even omitting certain notes. Example 71B shows us a simplified Amin11 voicing that omits the ♭3rd (C) and covers a narrower range of pitches (just over one octave) than Example 71A. This type of arpeggio is used extensively by Steve Vai.

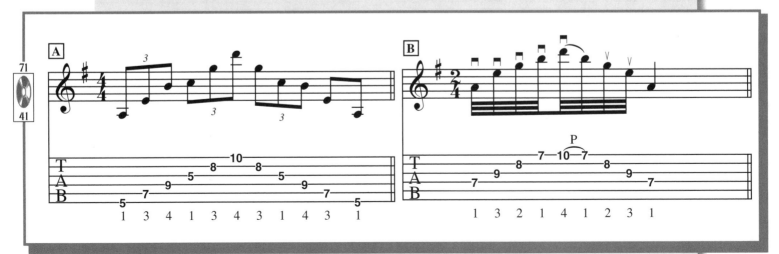

Example 72A is an AMaj9 arpeggio, which is AMaj7 plus the 9th. It's spelled 1–3–5–7–9 or A–C♯–E–G♯–B. Arpeggios like this not only sound beautiful and melodic, but they also enable us to play chords that normally would be challenging, if not impossible, on the guitar.

Example 72B slips and slides through a fun AMaj9 pattern. Shapes like this one can be found in the style of John Petrucci.

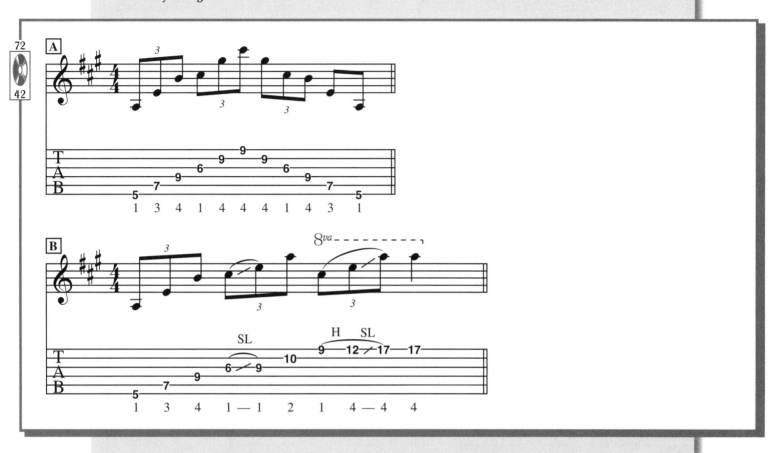

Now let's look at a challenging example that moves through several extended arpeggios within an A Minor progression. In order, they are GMaj13, Amin11, Dmin11, Emin11 and G9.

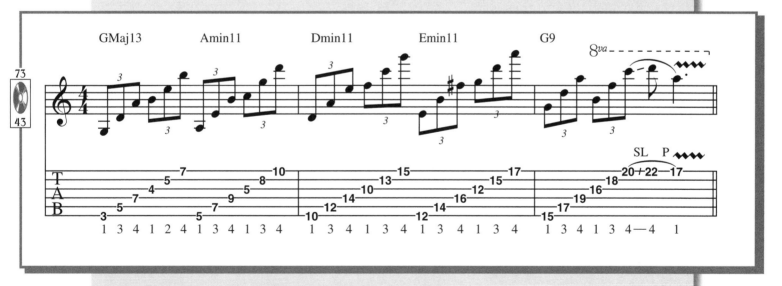

SWEEP PICKING

Sweep picking is the technique of raking, dragging, fanning or sweeping the pick across adjacent strings, taking advantage of consecutive downstrokes or upstrokes. This technique is most often applied to arpeggios to yield a speedy flurry of notes. Make one continuously fluid motion as opposed to individual strokes. Bouncing the pick is not allowed.

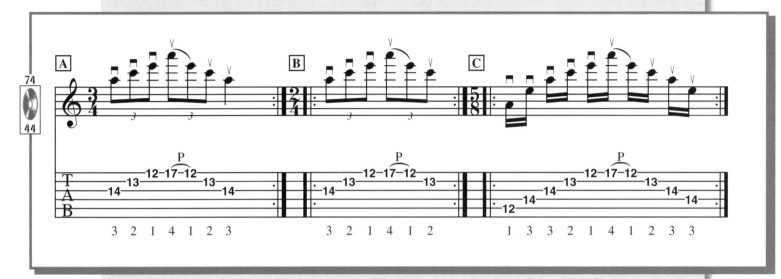

Now, let's sweep and shift our way around some four-string shapes over an Amin9 chord. The example below starts with an Amin11 arpeggio, then moves through a descending Dmin11, a G11, and finally back to the Amin11 one octave higher. It sounds harder than it really is, because the same pattern is used for each chord, and all of the notes are in the key of A Minor. If you read ahead and look before you leap, you should be able to keep the pattern going smoothly.

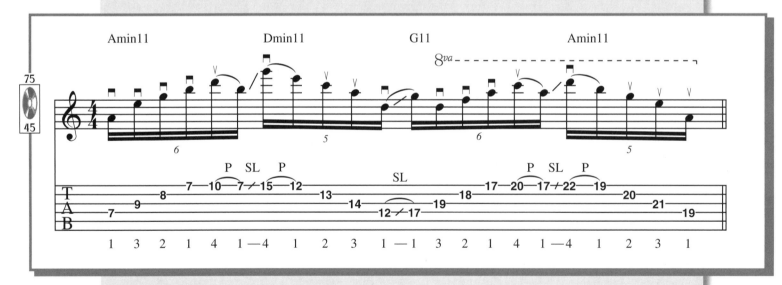

Example 76A introduces the E5 pattern, which is spelled 1–5 or E–B. It's the arpeggio equivalent of a *power chord,* a "one size fits all" pattern that works in many different situations. Because it has no 3rd, it works over both major and minor chords. Unless you're dealing with a diminished or augmented chord, chances are the 5 pattern will sound good.

Example 76B uses the same E5 pattern with different phrasing. This pattern is perfect for practicing your sweep picking technique because it has only one note per string.

Example 76C allows us to easily "connect the dots." It alternates between an E5 pattern and a D5 pattern.

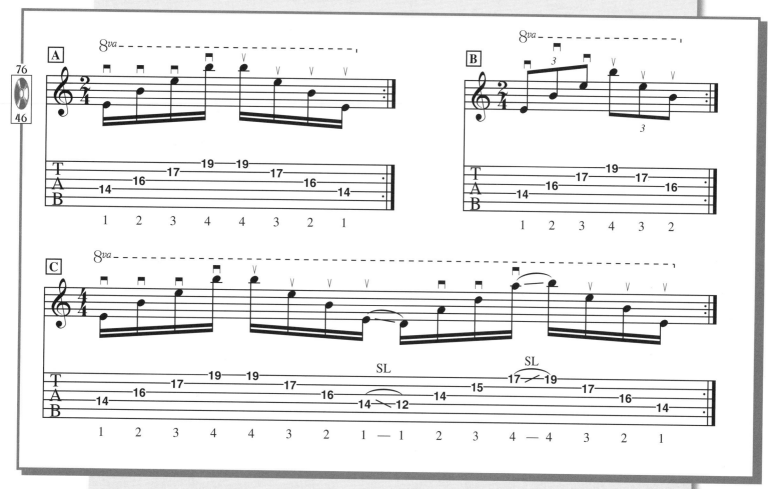

Example 77 features a new twist, the E5add9 arpeggio. Unlike extended chords, *add* chords are not built on 7th chords. E5add9 is spelled 1–5–9 or E–B–F#. Like the 5 pattern, 5add9 works over both major and minor chords, so long as there's not a ♭5, #5, ♭9 or #9 in the chord.

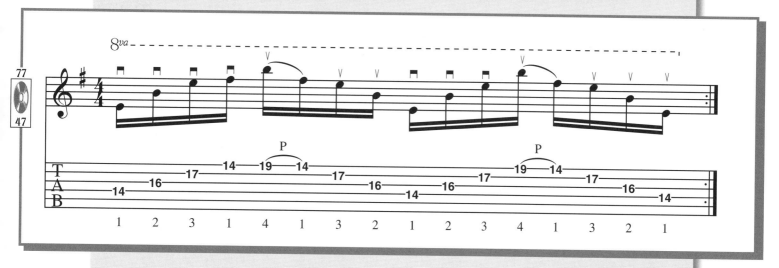

Now, we'll apply this pattern over an E Major chord. Ascending, we'll use the E5add9 pattern, and descending, we'll use a pedal tone through an E Major sequence to give us some more melody.

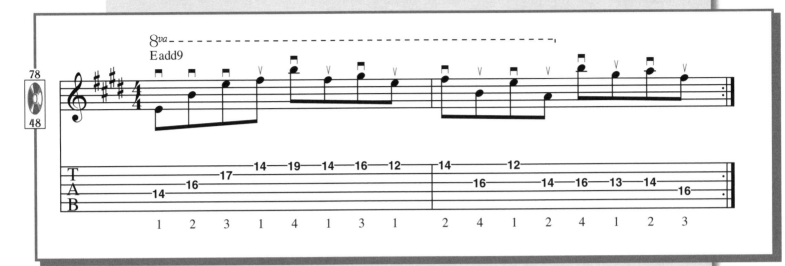

Let's find more ways to reinvent the 5add9 pattern. First, let's take a moment to learn a new type of chord. A *slash chord* is a chord that has a note other than the root as its bass (or lowest) note. Slash chords are written with the chord symbol, followed by a slash, followed by the name of the bass note. The slash chord F#11/E stands for an F#11 chord with an E in the bass. It would be spelled E–1–3–5–♭7–9–11 or E–F#–A#–C#–E–G#–B.

We'll begin with an ascending E5add9 lick over the F#11/E chord, similar to Example 77. When we descend, however, we'll change our melody to use the E Lydian mode. E Lydian uses a #4 or A#, which matches the F#11/E chord (using an A♮ would clash with A#, which is the 3rd of the chord.) Notice how changing this one note completely alters the sound of the lick. Normally, using A# would suggest the key of B Major. However, in this case, the harmony and melody both point toward E Lydian.

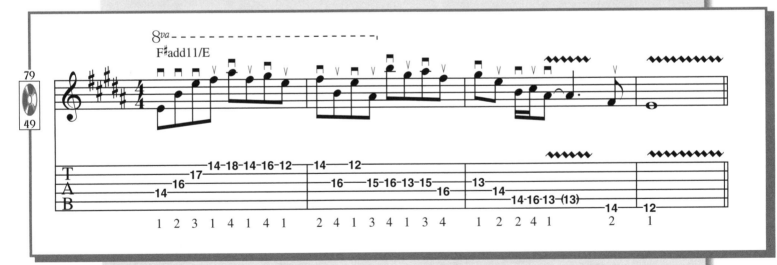

DIMINISHED 7TH ARPEGGIOS

Examples 80A and 80B are patterns for playing diminished 7th arpeggios. This type of arpeggio is a stylistic staple in classical, flamenco, neo-classical and shred guitar music. It's spelled 1–♭3–♭5–♭♭7. You'll hear these used by Yngwie Malmsteen, Michael Romeo, Al Di Meola and Joe Stump to name just a few.

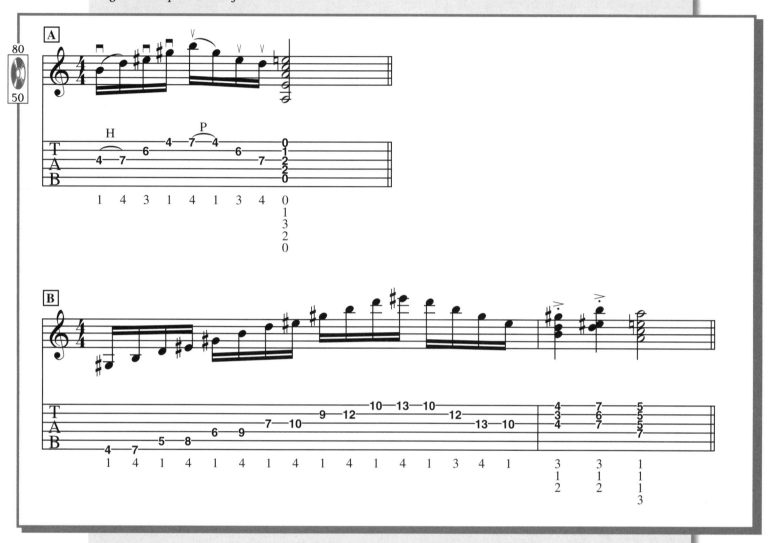

The following lick uses the rhythm from an old "tried and true" blues-rock lick, but incorporates a diminished arpeggio for an instant "doom and gloom" effect.

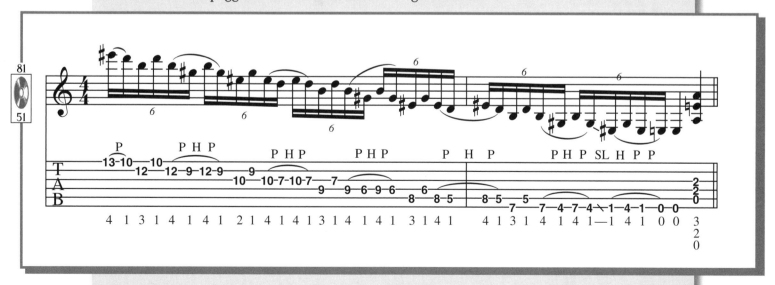

Example 82 uses an ascending series of overlapping diminished arpeggios. When moving up or down the neck in this manner, you'll discover that diminished 7th arpeggios repeat or overlap every four frets. That's because a diminished chord is *symmetrical;* every note in the arpeggio is the same interval (a minor 3rd) apart. So when you're ascending, move your 1st finger to where your 4th finger was to repeat the pattern. When descending, reverse the process and move your 4th finger to where your 1st finger was.

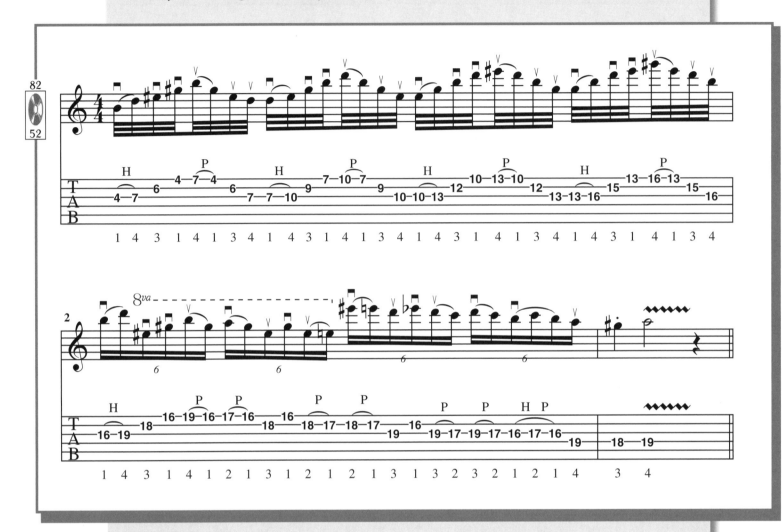

Example 83 eliminates the "middle" note in the diminished arpeggio. Doing so creates a symmetrical string-skipping pattern that allows for blistering speed. Take a careful look at the descending portion of this example, as it uses a different version of the diminished 7th pattern before going into a short, pedal-toned A Minor lick.

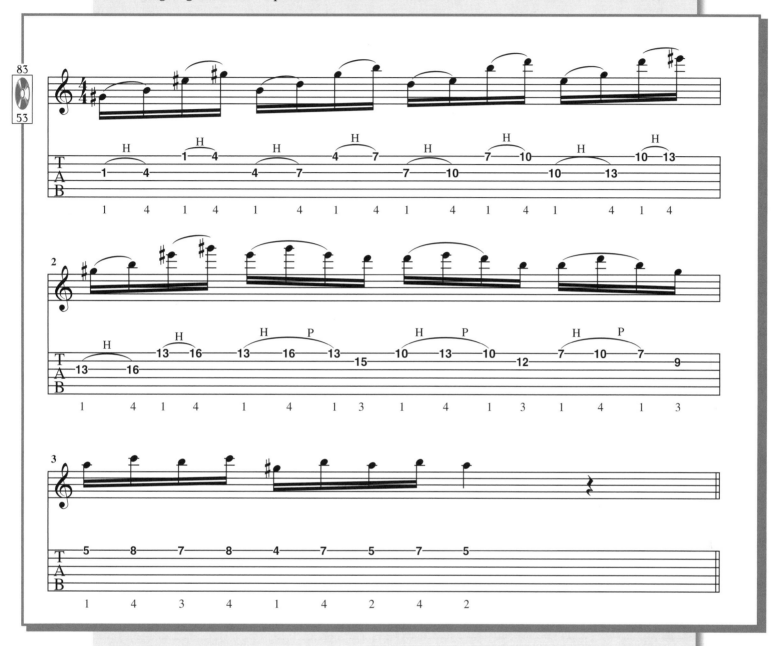

Example 84 brings to us a new shape for the diminished 7th arpeggio that resolves itself by descending a half step.

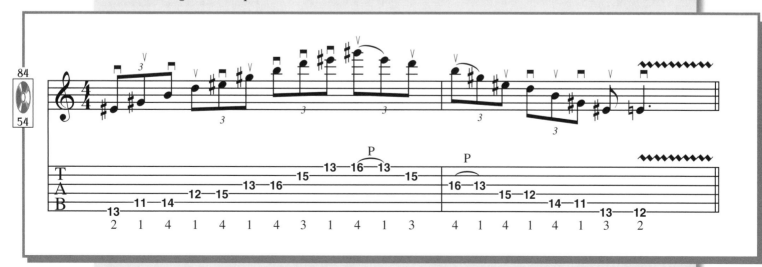

STRING-SKIPPING ARPEGGIO SHAPES

Examples 85 and 86 feature string-skipping arpeggio shapes. These are an interesting alternative to sweep picking. Keep in mind that skipping isn't just for arpeggios. It allows you to make greater leaps between intervals without having to make huge shifts in left-hand position. Once you are comfortable with the string-skipping exercises below, experiment with your own.

Example 85A is an A Major arpeggio with the root on the 4th string, and 85B is an E Major arpeggio with the root on the 5th string.

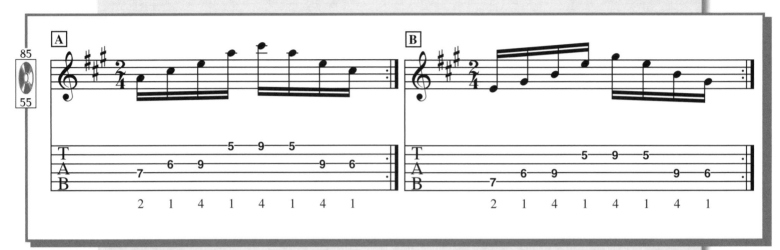

Example 86A and 86B demonstrate minor arpeggios rooted on the 4th and 5th strings respectively. Example 86A is A Minor and Example 86B is E Minor.

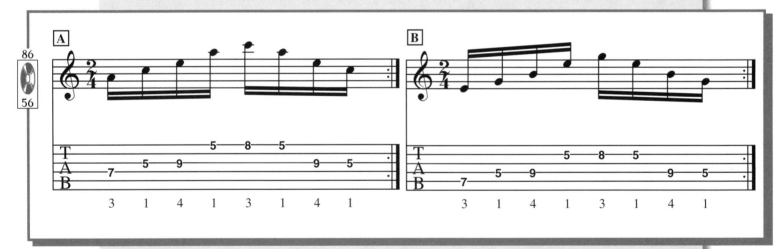

Following is an *etude*, or study, in string-skipping arpeggios in A Minor. Take your time and gradually work up to lightning speed. Here's a hint for playing the first four bars: The arpeggio on beats 3 and 4 is the same shape and fingering as the arpeggio on beats 1 and 2, simply moved to a different string and/or fret.

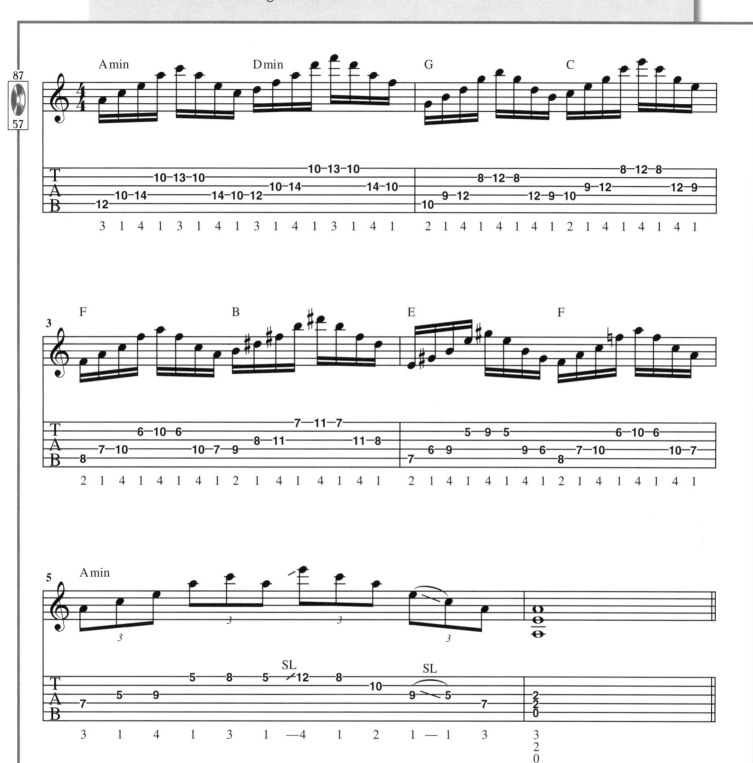

FOUR- AND SIX-NOTE PATTERNS

Example 88 begins with ascending and overlapping four-note groupings. After reaching the top of the pattern, we work our way back down again using descending, overlapping four-note groups. Passages such as this can be found in the playing style of the legendary Michael Schenker (guitarist for the Scorpions, UFO and the Michael Schenker Group).

Keep your right arm, wrist, and hand as relaxed as possible and adhere to a strict down-up-down-up (alternate) picking pattern.

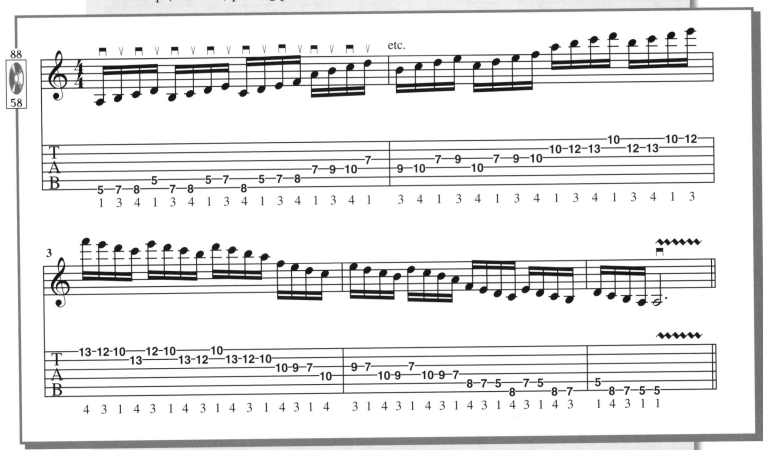

The following example features a cool-sounding melodic *contour* or sequencing of the notes in a particular pattern or scale. Once you become familiar with this phrasing pattern, try applying it to other three-note-per-string licks that are already in your trick bag. With a little patience, you can have this one up to blistering speed in no time.

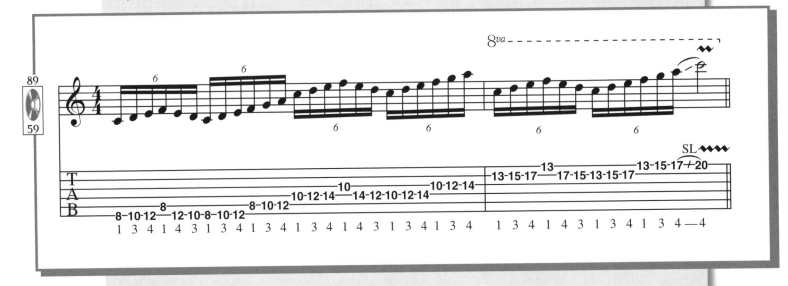

MAJOR 7TH ARPEGGIO

The *major 7th* arpeggio is spelled 1–3–5–7. Example 90 starts off with a jazz or fusion-styled CMaj7 lick followed by a tasty little bend and release and some descending C Major triads.

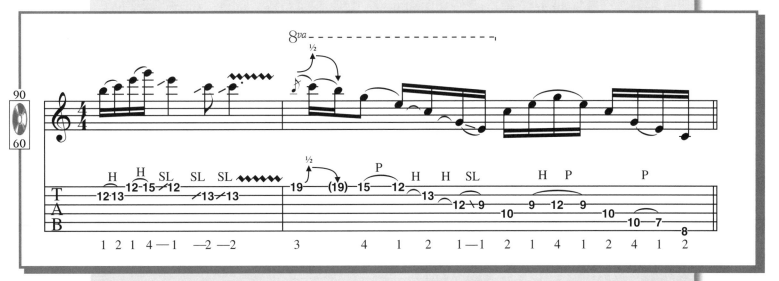

Once you get this next one up and running, you won't want to stop playing it. This fluid-sounding lick is a series of D Major arpeggios that uses several of the tricks we've learned so far: tapping, sweeping and string skipping. It would make a great ending to a song or solo.

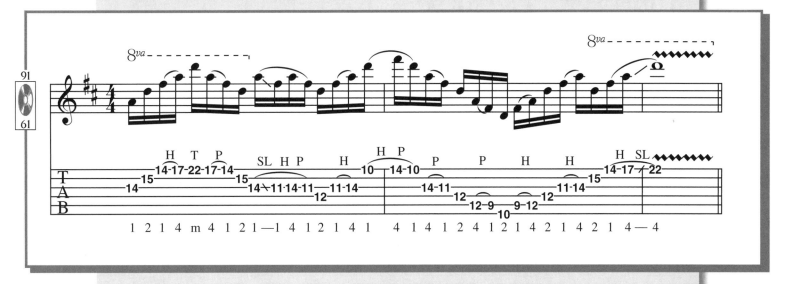

ASCENDING DIMINISHED 7TH ARPEGGIOS

Example 92 is a really cool and twisted lick right out of the trick bag of players like George Lynch and Kirk Hammett of Metallica. It's simply a series of major triads, but each of the triads starts on a different note of an E Diminished 7 arpeggio. The result is something right out of an old-school horror flick. Notice the heavy vibrato on the ending E(♭5) double stop.

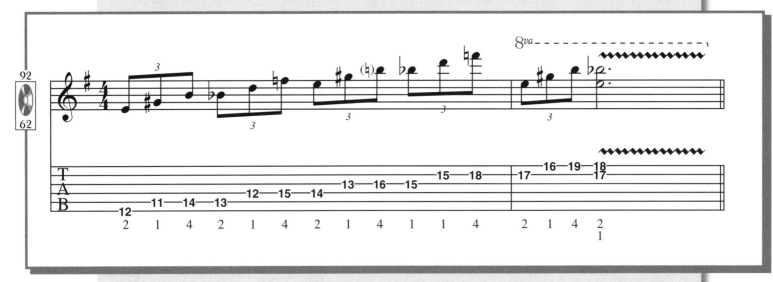

LOOPING WITH A AEOLIAN AND B LOCRIAN

In the following example, we'll use A Aeolian and B Locrian to *loop* or "U-turn" starting with an ascending line in the middle of the neck, running up to the 12th position and then moving all the way back down to the 5th position for a climactic low A on the 6th string.

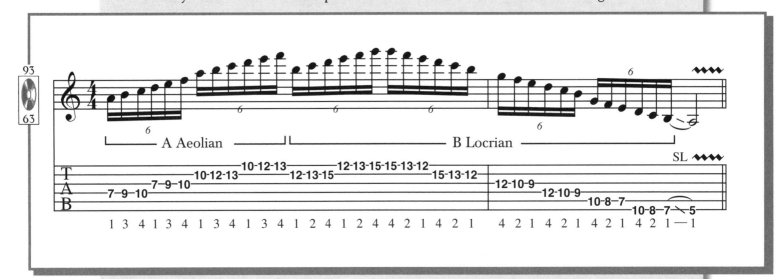

SYMMETRICAL SHAPES APPLIED

Example 94 is a lick similar to the styles of guitar innovators Eddie Van Halen and the late "Dimebag" Darrell of Pantera and Damageplan. Guitar magazines often feature licks like this with explanations of the theory behind them, along the lines of "one line is taken from the major scale and another from the Mixolydian, blah blah blah." The truth is, most guitarists don't really think about the theory when playing a pattern like this. It's just a symmetrical shape that sounds good when played across the neck (and it never hurts to top it off with a good old-fashion blues lick as is the case here).

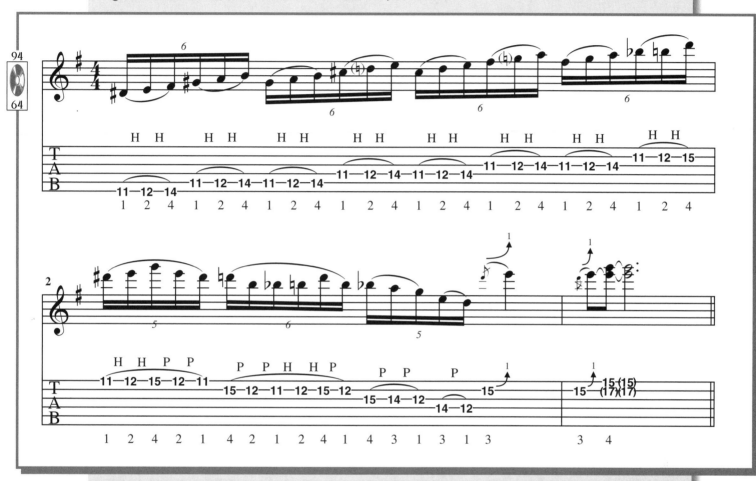

Example 95 is an example of *re-sequencing;* the order of notes in the pattern is jumbled up, both ascending and descending. This gives a much more interesting sound than simply running the scale in order.

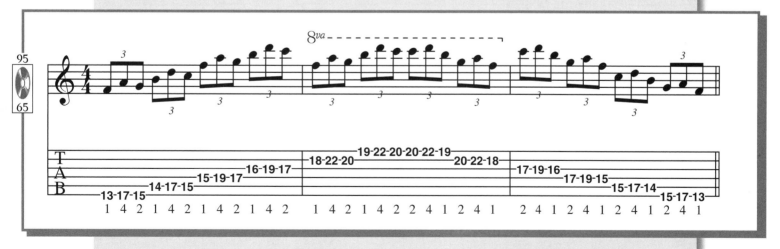

MORE LICKS

The following example is a raging slab of metal mayhem from the neo-classical school of shredding. It starts out with a short, ascending E Phrygian Altered run, moves into descending pedal tone licks in A Harmonic Minor and ends way down low with a *divebomb* (downward bend using the whammy bar) of the open 6th string.

Remember, *pedal tones* (see page 19) are a melodic device found in many different genres but most strongly associated with classical music. A pedal tone is a note that repeats throughout a musical phrase while the other notes around it rise or fall. For example, in the melody F–E–F–D–F–C–F–B–F–A–F–G♯, the pedal tone is F.

Here's an example that actually uses two pedal tones. In measure 1, F is the pedal tone on beats 1 and 3, while B is the pedal tone on beats 2 and 4. The descending lick in measure 2 uses chromatic notes and is reminiscent of *bebop,* a melodically complex style of jazz.

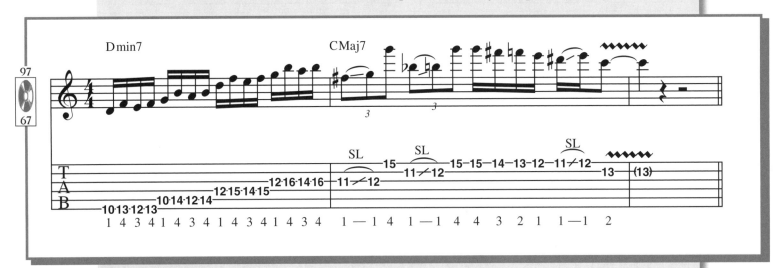

TAPPING

Okay all you finger-tapping maniacs, here's the section you've been waiting for. Let's jump right in and look at a blistering ascending and descending lick that uses overlapping octave patterns. It ends with a single-string run up to a tapped high A.

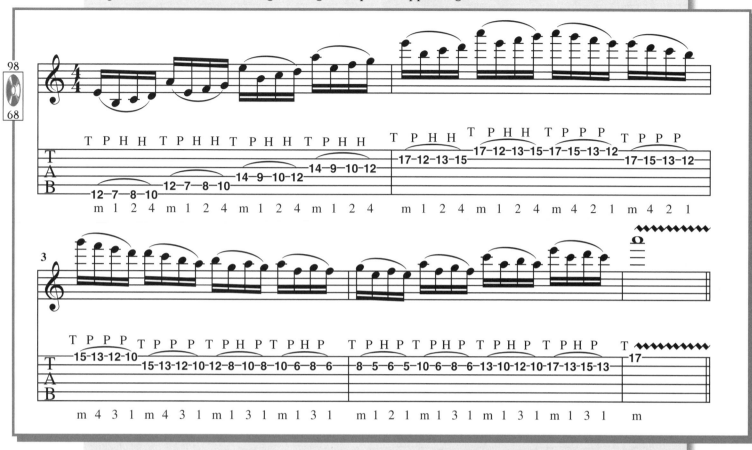

Example 99 is in the style of Symphony X's Michael Romeo. It consists entirely of tapped notes and hammer-ons. The first note of each ascending line is played using the *hammer-on from nowhere* technique, also known as a *ghost tap*. The note is simply hammered-on with the left hand with no right-hand pick attack or pluck whatsoever. Take your time and keep your technique smooth and fluid. The desired sound is liquid and seamless.

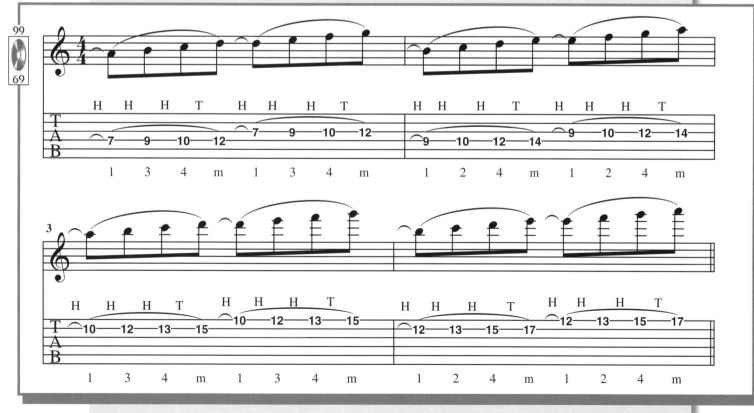

The next example takes shredding to a whole new level by adding tapped notes to sweep-picked arpeggios. Pay close attention to the picking instructions and the exact location of the pull-offs. These details become very important as you try to build speed.

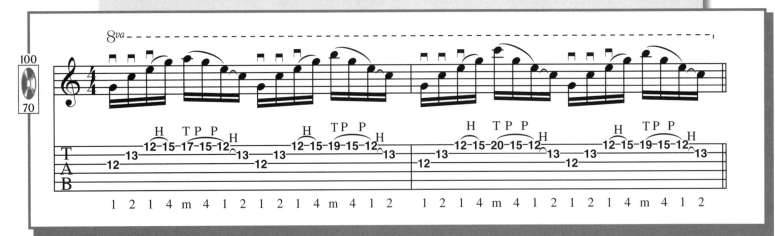

Example 101 is a rapid-fire tapped/legato blues-based lick using the E Blues scale. There are some tapped notes that are then slid and also some legato position-shifting slides that add some "grease" to this one.

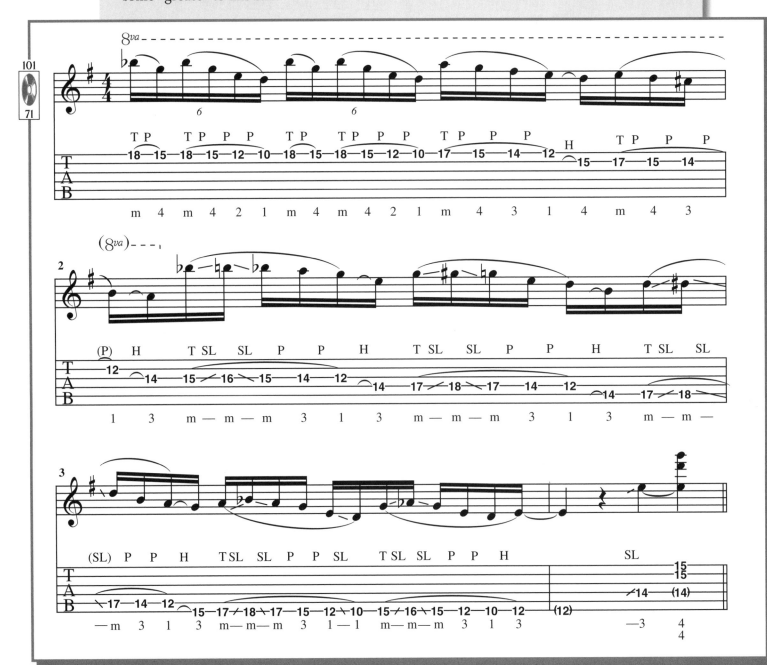

Example 102 is a legato flurry of sixteenth notes in E Minor Pentatonic. Watch those legato slides and shifts!

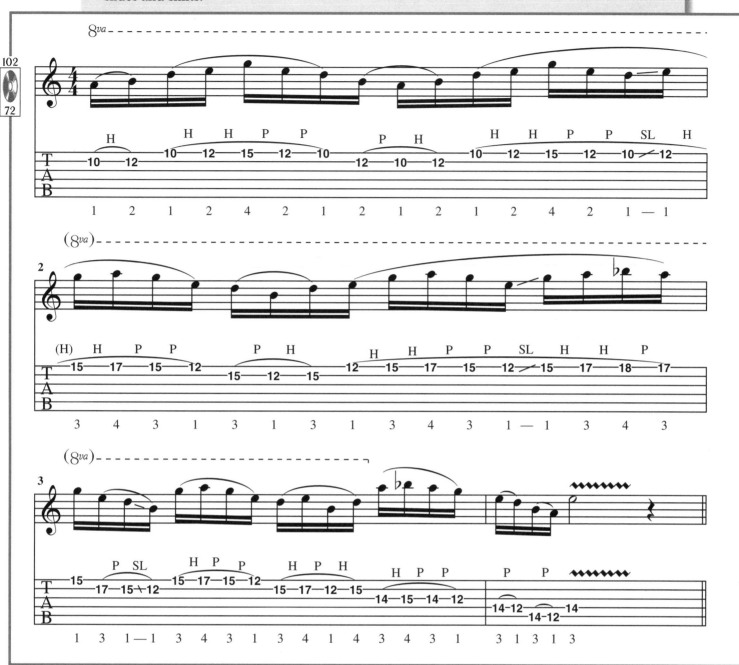

Here's a descending series of diminished tapped arpeggios. Notice how the pattern is completely symmetrical in shape, making it easy to work up to a blistering speed. Also note the hammer-on from nowhere technique used here. Your left-hand finger should move to the next string to sound the hammer-on before your right-hand tapping finger moves to the new string. It's a cool technique to squeeze one more extra note out of a run or sequence.

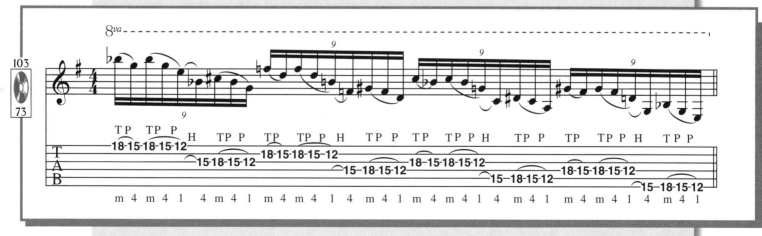

MODAL ARPEGGIOS

In this chapter, we'll discover more substitutes for common arpeggios. Most players stay within their comfort zone when using arpeggios. Usually, they stick to the "stock" major and minor shapes and patterns. The *modal arpeggios* that follow are more exotic and colorful.

Let's begin by analyzing the modes to determine which scale degrees give them their distinctive color, personality and flavor. If we concentrate on these particular scale degrees, we'll squeeze the most out of the mode without having to play every single note in the scale. We'll also learn how the modes can substitute for major or minor sounds in a solo or chord progression.

DORIAN

Let's start with the Dorian mode in A, spelled A–B–C–D–E–F♯–G or 1–2–♭3–4–5–6–♭7.

The first arpeggio we'll look at (Example 104A) is spelled 1–♭3–5–♭7–9–11 with the root on the 5th string at the 12th fret. This triplet pattern can easily be played using either sweep/economy picking or alternate picking.

Example 104B has the root on the 6th string, 17th fret. This time, we'll include the natural sixth (an important interval responsible for the Dorian sound). The pattern here is 1–5–♭7–11–13–9 or A–E–G–D–F♯–B. Can you hear the difference?

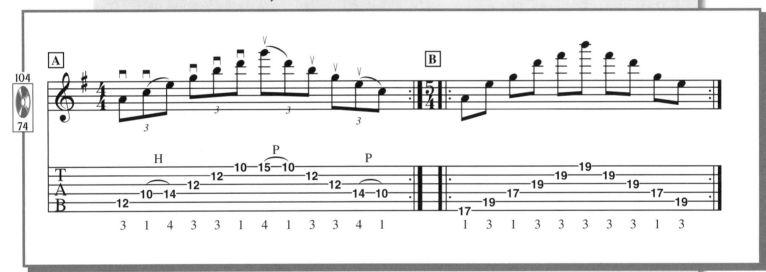

Combining this modal approach with some position shifts and sequencing will make things more interesting and exotic. This is an unconventional lick:

MIXOLYDIAN

Next up, we'll use the Mixolydian mode in an arpeggio. This example is in D Mixolydian, spelled D–E–F♯–G–A–B–C or 1–2–3–4–5–6–♭7.

Our first Mixolydian arpeggio (Example 106A) is spelled 1–3–5–♭7–9–11–13 or D–F♯–A–C–E–G–B. Our second Mixolydian shape (Example 106B) has a 6th string root. It sounds great over a dominant 7th chord.

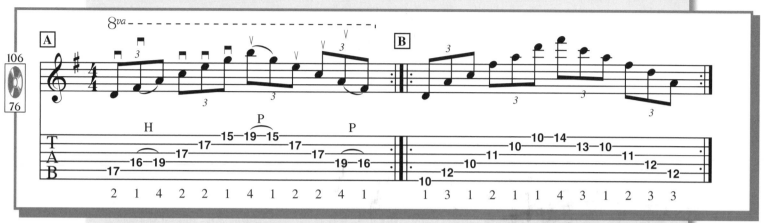

LYDIAN

The next example explores the C Lydian mode (C–D–E–F♯–G–A–B). The Lydian mode gets its unique sound from the ♯4 (or ♯11). The first Lydian arpeggio (Example 107A) is spelled 1–3–5–7–9–♯11–13. It's a really great pattern for sweeping, as the left hand changes fingers with each string change, and each string is easily muted when moving to the next. The second pattern (Example 107B) draws directly from the ♯11 chord, sometimes called the *Lydian chord*.

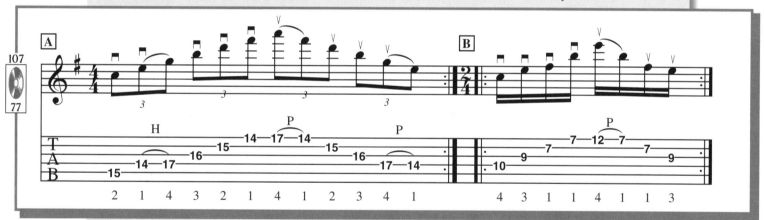

SUS2, DOM7 AND SUS4

To expand our sonic palette, let's wrap things up with a couple of often-overlooked arpeggio types. Here we have arpeggios for sus2, dom7 and sus4 chords. Suspended chords can be used as substitutions for either major or minor chords because they do not contain a 3rd (the interval that determines whether a chord is major or minor).

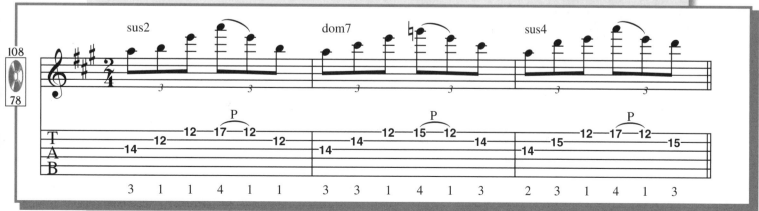

OVERLAPPING MINOR AND MAJOR SHAPES

Up to this point, we've covered a lot of music theory. The danger of learning all this theory is that we sometimes feel bound to the rules and that all of our note choices must be *diatonic* or "in the key" when we are soloing and improvising. While it's *usually* a good idea to play "inside," there are a lot of interesting sounds available by finding loopholes in the rules.

OVERLAPPING MINOR SHAPES

First, we'll examine the different minor scales. Example 109 on the following page illustrates the *caged* or *boxed* shapes for the minor pentatonic, Aeolian/natural minor, Dorian, Phrygian and Locrian scales. Notice there are places where they all line up or overlap. They all share the same root, ♭3rd, 4th, 5th and ♭7th. In other words, each of these different minor scales overlaps with every note in the minor pentatonic scale. This explains why the minor pentatonic scale is so widely used. Every note within this scale is either a strong chord tone (1, ♭3, 5) or can be bent up to a strong chord tone (4 to 5; ♭7 to the root). It is almost impossible to make a bad note choice when using the minor pentatonic scale.

Because of these shared or overlapping notes, the different minor scales can be blended or combined together to make *hybrids*. This is especially true when soloing over a one- or two-chord progression, or *vamp*, where there is not much harmonic movement.

By combining different scales, you end up with a wider range of flavors and colors from which to choose. Joe Satriani and others refer to this concept as *pitch axis*. The pitch axis is the central tone or reference point that stays the same as you weave in and out of other scales or keys.

Another common strategy among instrumentalists, such as the great Steve Vai, is to have the rhythm guitars drop out during a solo section so the lead guitarist can improvise accompanied only by bass and drums. This sparse backing track allows for a freer choice of notes. You don't need to worry about clashing with the other guitarist's chord tones; your only limitation is sounding good with the bassist, who is usually either playing the root or repeating a riff.

Feel free to experiment with stopping and hovering on all the many different tones you have to chose from. Later in this section, we'll see some examples of hybrid runs.

A final word of advice before moving on: When substituting one scale for another, think in terms of mood and color. Let's say you are soloing over a minor progression and the Aeolian mode sounds too dark. Try lightening the mood with the Dorian mode, which has a more uplifting or jazzy sound due to the natural 6th. On the other hand, if you wanted something darker and more exotic than Aeolian, you might try the Phrygian mode with its flatted 2nd. Try this type of experimentation and substitution with everything you play.

Minor Pentatonic

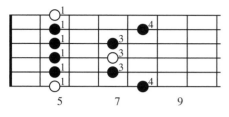

Aeolian/Natural Minor

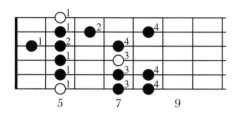

Dorian

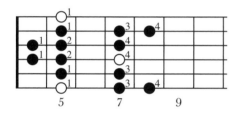

Phrygian

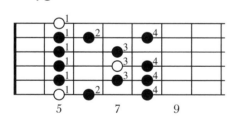

Locrian

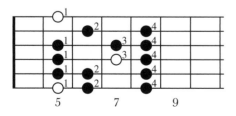

OVERLAPPING MAJOR SHAPES

Now, let's apply the same concept to scales and modes that contain a major 3rd. The charts below show the major pentatonic, Ionian/major, Mixolydian, Lydian and Phrygian Dominant scales. At first glance, the similarities may take a moment or two to see, unlike the square-looking minor shapes.

Just as we saw with the minor scales, the majors may be combined and cross-pollinated into all sorts of twisting, turning licks.

Feel free to experiment with any of the major scales and modes. Many rock players get bogged down in repetitive minor-key soloing and songwriting. It's good to break out of that rut and try to spark some new creativity. Explore the sound and feel of the Mixolydian and Lydian modes, as they're more open and less "boxed in" sounding than the Ionian mode. They're a little less bright and slightly bittersweet.

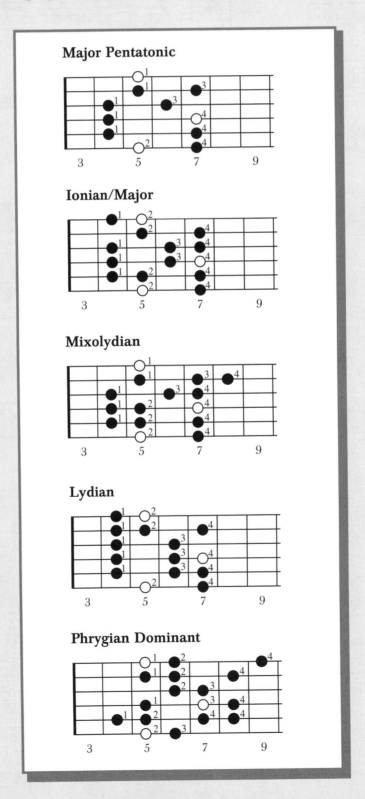

THINKING INSIDE

In this chapter, we'll learn to see the "shapes within the shapes." We'll look deeper into patterns we already know to unlock new patterns for scales and arpeggios. This knowledge will free you from feeling trapped inside your "boxes" and help you to visualize how the fretboard locks together. It will open you up to all kinds of new melodic possibilities.

First, we'll take a look at the box and extended patterns for D Minor (D–E–F–G–A–B♭–C). By starting these same patterns on the 5th string, beginning with G (the 4th degree of the scale), we'll find we have new shapes for G Dorian (G–A–B♭–C–D–E–F).

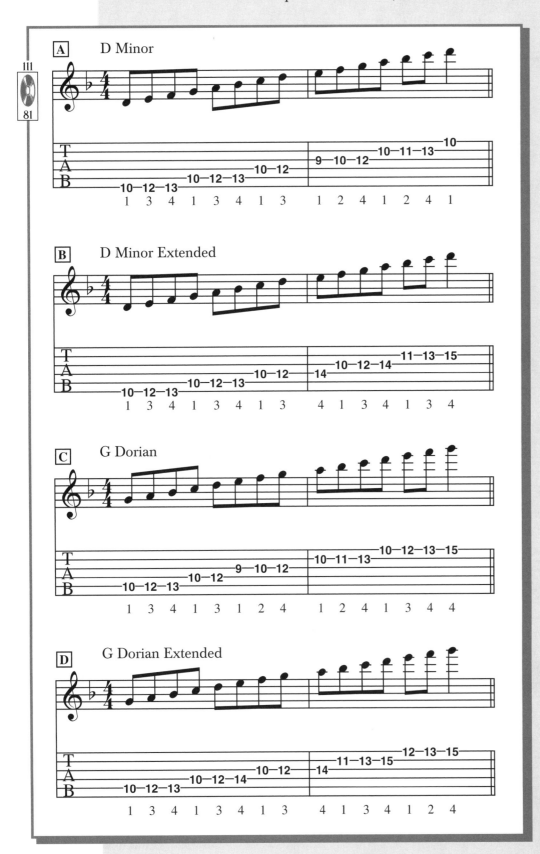

The patterns in the previous examples have "hidden" arpeggio shapes within them. Below are some of these shapes; you'll find they lie nicely under your fingertips.

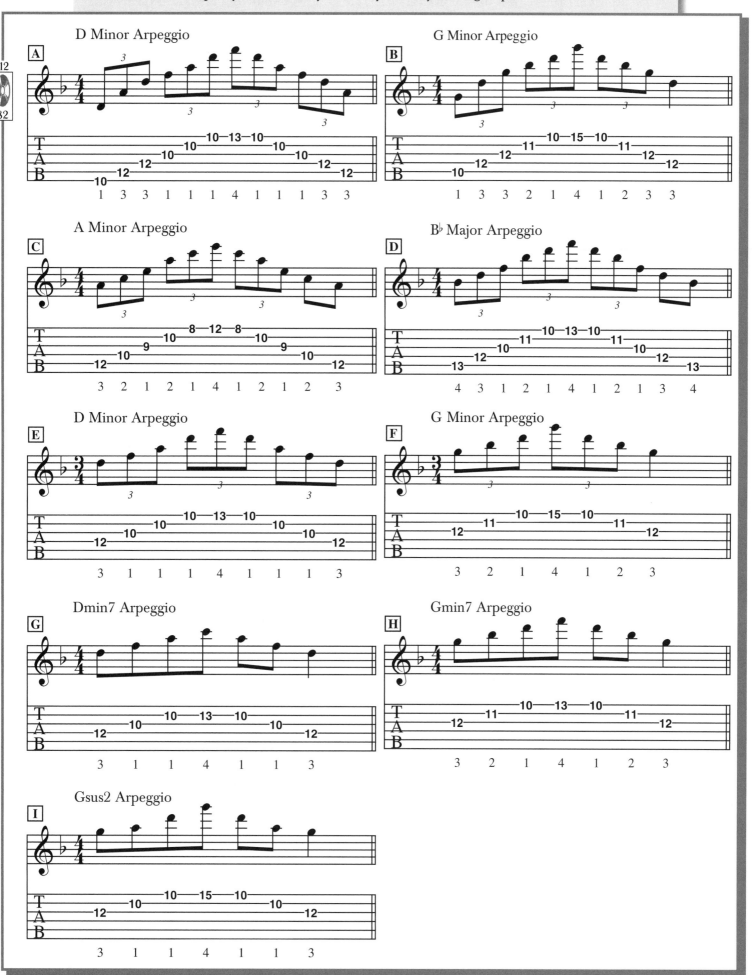

Examples 113A and 113B demonstrate how one note can change the flavor of an arpeggio (the high G in Example 113A and the high F in Example 113B). Examples 113C–113E illustrate how one arpeggio can progress directly into another, creating slick-sounding melodic sequences.

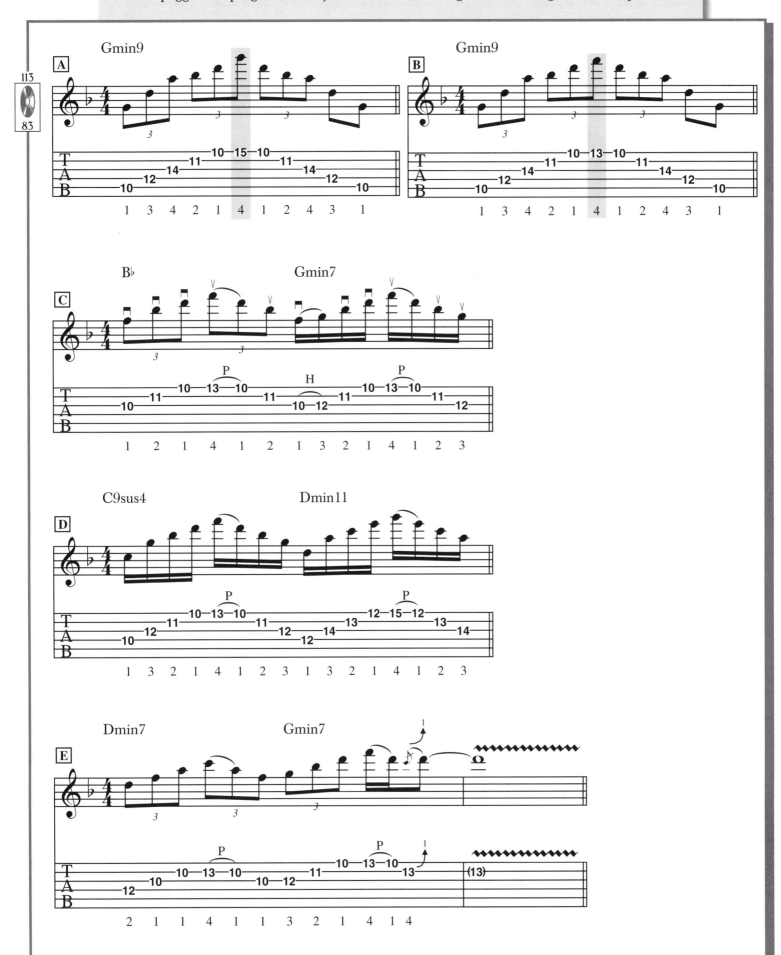

The example below moves through all of the diatonic triads within the key of D Minor.

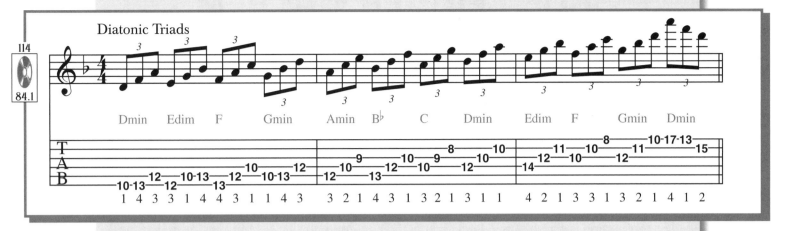

The following example uses diatonic 7th arpeggios to add some color: Dmin7, Gmin7, Amin7 and finally Dmin7/F.

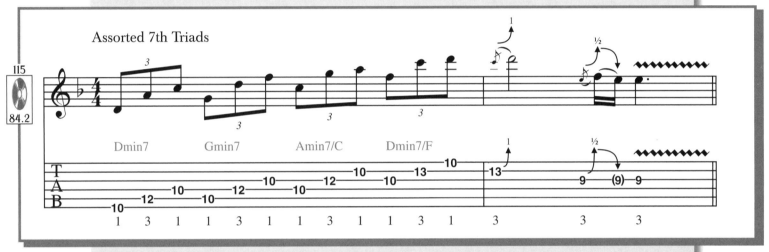

The final example in this section extends the concept further by adding some chromatic color (C♯) to the D Blues scale, along with some string-skipped pedal tones in the style of Eric Johnson.

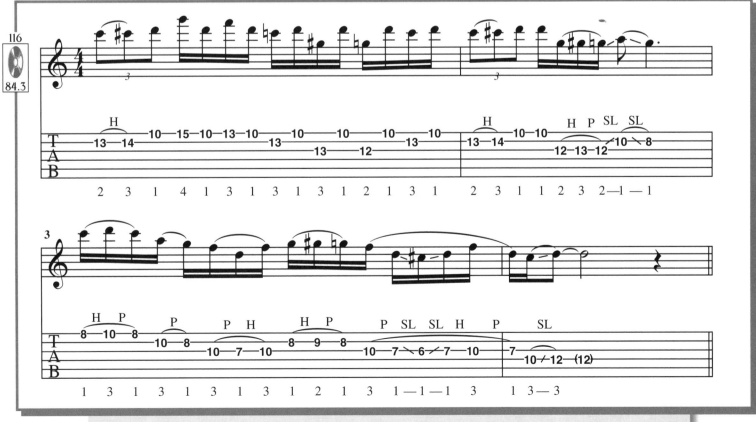

MULTI-FINGER MAYHEM
(EXPLORING MULTI-FINGER TAPPING)

Multi-finger tapping is exactly what it sounds like. It involves tapping with multiple fingers as opposed to the traditional method of only using one finger.

With single-finger tapping, some guitarists use their 1st finger, cupping the pick with their palm or 2nd finger, while others tap with the 2nd finger. Using the 2nd finger allows you to quickly switch back and forth between picking and tapping.

For this section, you won't need a pick at all. We're going to start tapping with three of the right-hand fingers. This technique is used by Stanley Jordan, Jennifer Batten, Michael Romeo and many others.

A word of caution: Take it slow and easy! If you haven't experimented with this particular technique before, you can easily wind up with some very tender fingertips. Avoid the temptation to play until your fingers are sore.

The following example uses what are known as *mirror shapes*. This means that both hands will be fretting the same shape in different portions of the neck. This is very common in the world of multi-finger tapping. Examples 117A and 177B use the same notes, arranged differently. 177A combines both hands together, while 177B separates the hands so you can really see the identical shapes. The two hands combine to outline a Dsus4 arpeggio. The left hand plays D–G–D (1–4–1) while the right hand plays A–D–A (5–1–5).

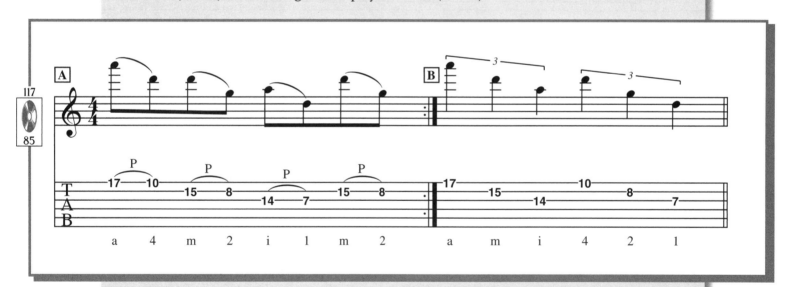

The right-hand fingers are named after the Spanish terms used in classical guitar notation.

(p) *Pulgar* — Thumb
(i) *Indice* — Index
(m) *Medio* — Middle
(a) *Anular* — Ring

Now, we'll extend the range of this pattern by descending through two octaves. You'll notice that the patterns continue to mirror each other as they descend. It's still just one big Dsus4 arpeggio.

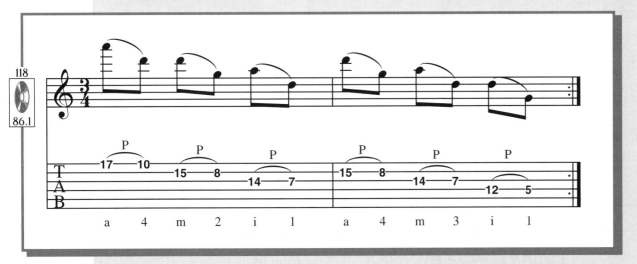

Let's apply this pattern to a chord progression. The left hand will hold down small chord shapes on the first three strings and shift through the changes, while the right hand keeps the same triad. The movement of the progression comes from the left hand alone. The left-hand chord shapes are really just the top three strings of the full chord voicings for D, E Minor, A and G.

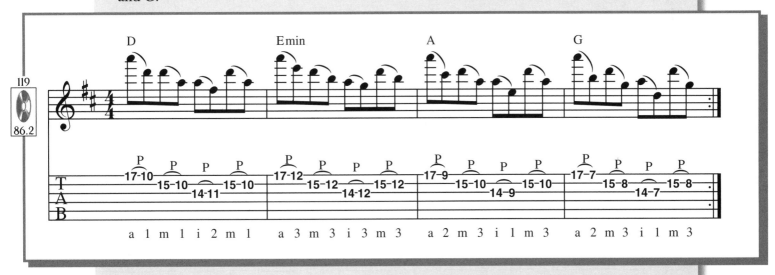

The next example has more of a "rock" sound. It uses the classic chord progression E Minor, D, C and B. Unlike the previous example, this time your right hand will move too, progressing down the neck along with your left hand.

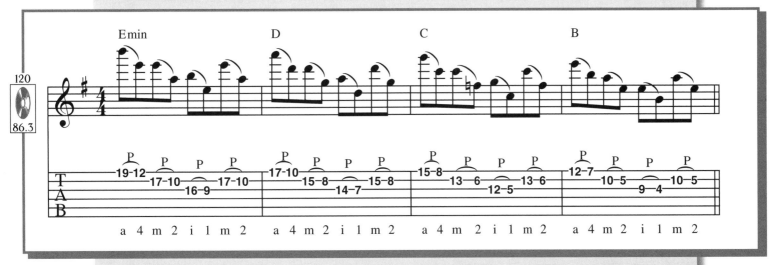

The following etude uses multi-finger tapping exclusively. No pick is necessary for this one. In the Intro or A section, you'll notice the use of open strings. Only your right hand moves here, while your left hand remains in position.

To sound the open D chords, simply strum the strings with the fingers of your right hand.

At the start of the B section, your right hand remains stationary while your left hand adds and subtracts the major 7th (C♯). Then, we move into a section of cascading chord changes. Your left hand shifts to form the chord shape, while your right hand drives and provides the motion.

The C section wraps things up nicely with a two-octave descent through matching chord shapes, ending with a huge-sounding Dsus2/A chord.

Now you're more than ready to experiment and create your own multi-finger tapping runs.

E MAJOR ETUDE

This solo etude is divided into two big sections, A and B. It is based around an E Major tonality and is in the style of guitar greats such as Neal Schon (Journey), Joe Satriani and John Petrucci.

So much of the rock and shred guitar vocabulary is based on the dark and heavy minor keys that it's difficult sometimes to confidently play through major key progressions. Solos in major keys can be wonderfully soaring and triumphant musical moments.

This etude has a couple of moments that deserve special mention. In section A, watch out for the string skipping that outlines the E Major chord in measure 1 and the sweeps and flutters that follow in measure 2. In section B, pay special attention to the legato phrasing in measure 11 followed by the one-note-per-string arpeggio action in measure 12.

This etude is all about combining feel and finesse with technique. Be mindful of the rhythmic phrasing of the melodies and pay attention to the bends and vibrato. The *natural harmonics* (high-pitched notes played by lightly resting the left-hand finger on the string, rather than pressing it down to the fret) in the last two measures yield an extremely high-pitched E5 chord. Paying attention to the little details will really make this etude sing.

Practice the 1st guitar part (Gtr. I) along with Track 89, which contains the second guitar part (Gtr. II) only.

Photo by Timothy Ryan Phelps

Joe Satriani (b. 1956) is best known for his virtuoso playing on his solo albums (such as Surfing with the Alien *and* Flying in a Blue Dream*) and as founder of the G3 concert tours that have showcased guitar legends Steve Vai, Eric Johnson, Kenny Wayne Shepherd, Yngwie Malmsteen and others. He has toured with such diverse artists as Mick Jagger and Deep Purple. He is also a legendary guitar educator whose students include Steve Vai, Kirk Hammett, Larry LaLonde, David Bryson and Charlie Hunter.*

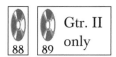

E MAJOR ETUDE

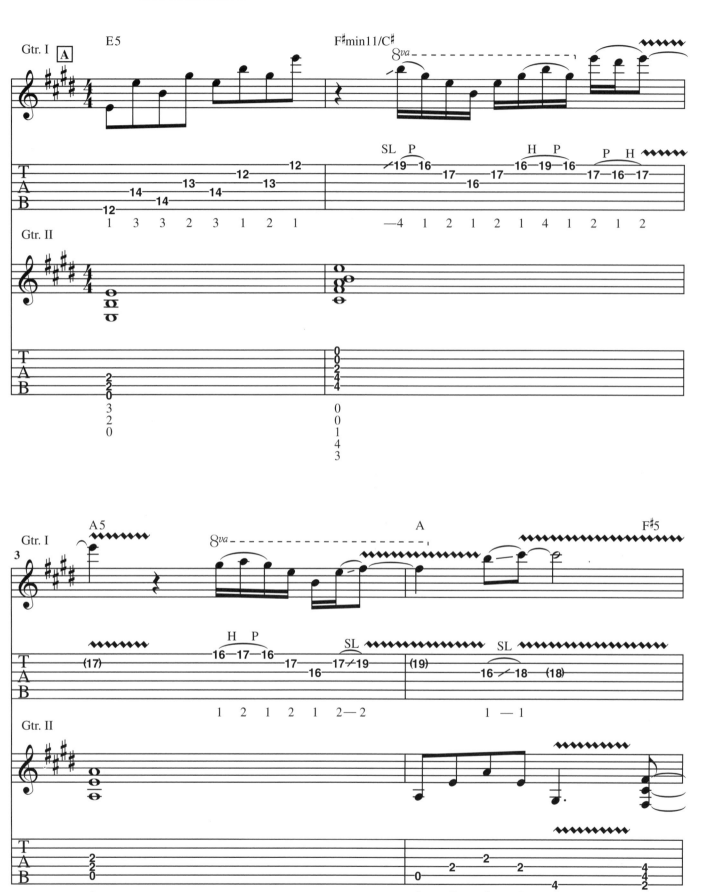

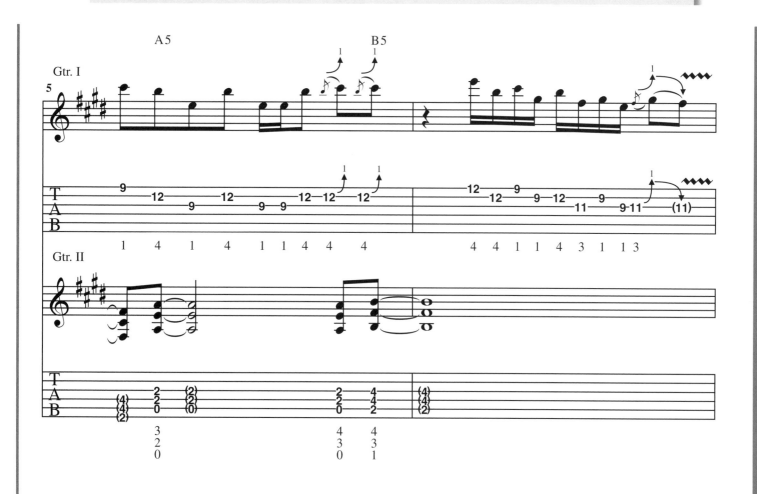

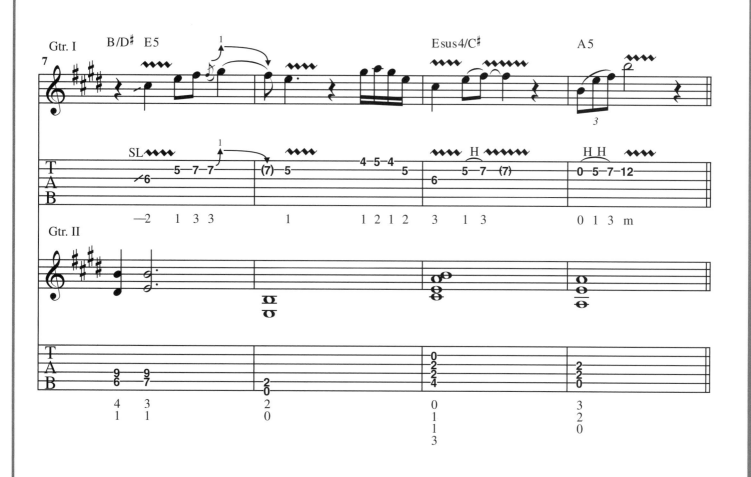

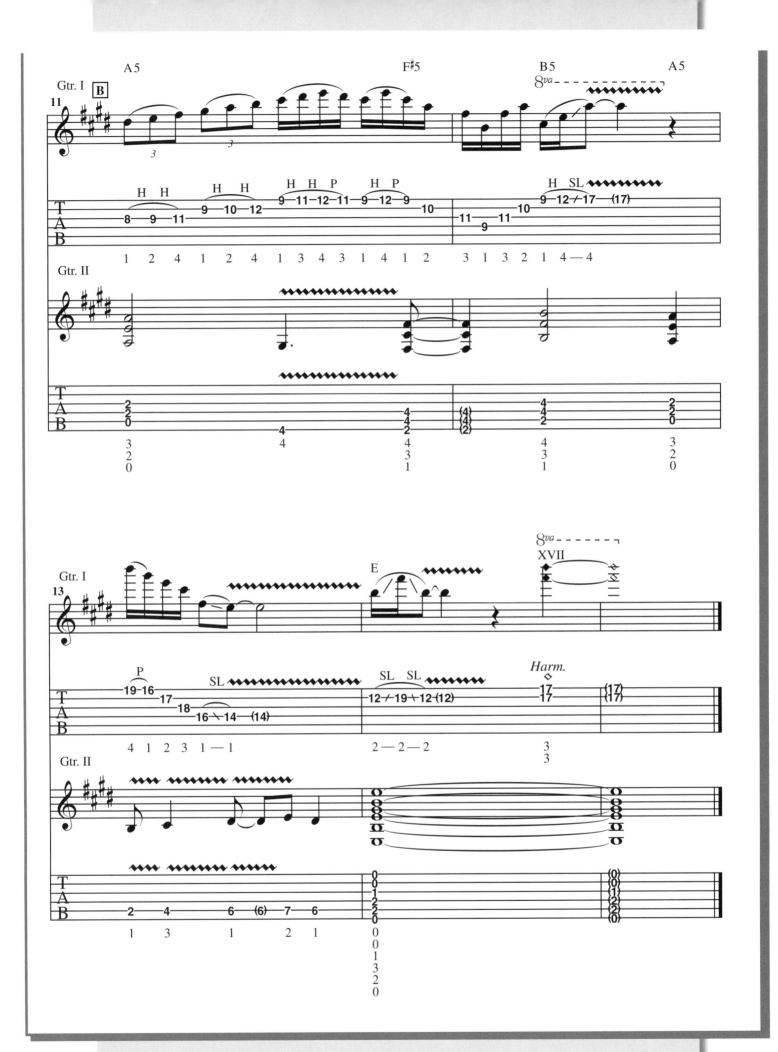

C♯ MINOR ETUDE

In contrast to the "E Major Etude," the "C♯ Minor Etude" will explore more melodic and moody territory. Here are a few of this etude's defining moments:

- The descending triplet line that starts the 6th measure of section A.

- The ascending AMaj7 arpeggios in the first measure of section B and in section C.

- The triplets that outline EMaj7 in the first measure of section C.

- The double stops in measure 5. These create a melodic fill that is reminiscent of what a blues pianist might do.

- In measure 7, beat 4 is emphasized by the use of an *artificial harmonic* (*Art. Harm.*, also known as a "pinch" harmonic, squeal or ping). Artificial harmonics are achieved by digging into the string a little harder than normal, attacking the string with the pick and the side of the thumb simultaneously.

Notation for the rhythm guitar part has been provided for this etude so you can take note of the techniques used. Always search for a fresh twist to put into your rhythm playing.

Practice the 1st guitar part (Gtr. I) along with Track 91, which contains the second guitar part only.

Steve Vai (b. 1960) is an influential virtuoso guitarist. As a teenager, he studied with Joe Satriani, and then went on to attend the Berklee College of Music. His impressive transcription and sight-reading skills earned him a gig with Frank Zappa's band. He gained a wider audience in the mid-1980s as a member of David Lee Roth's group. Vai's playing is characterized by technical facility and deep knowledge of music theory, and he played a big role in popularizing the 7-string guitar. He tours with his own group and with Joe Satriani as part of G3.

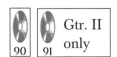

C# MINOR ETUDE

C DORIAN ETUDE

Phrasing is the order of the day here. Good phrasing will make this Dorian-based solo sound slinky and sexy. Too many players (especially in the beginning stages of acquiring speed and technique) simply open the flood gates and barrage the listener with thousands of notes at blinding speeds. They want to "wow" and impress the listener, but too often it can have the opposite effect. Take note of the feel, mood and tempo of any given piece of music. Let the music breathe and flow. Solos with musicality, feel, touch and melody are usually the most memorable. Phrasing is like having a conversation with the listener using notes, melody, timing and placement instead of words. For examples of good phrasing, listen to horn players, because they have to breathe between (and sometimes even during) phrases.

The opening descending flurry of sixteenth-note sextuplets twists and spirals downward, combining C Dorian and the minor blues scale into a swooping one-and-a-half-step bend on the 6th string. In the first bar of the B section, you'll find our minor 7th triad ascending for three octaves. From there, you'll encounter assorted slide shifts and bends that really help this solo speak to the listener.

Practice the 1st guitar part (Gtr. I) along with Track 93, which contains the second guitar part only.

Photo by Bastone/Courtesy of Star File Photo, Inc.

Eric Johnson (b. 1954) hails from Austin, Texas. He is renowned as a guitar virtuoso with a sweet, sustaining tone. He recorded his first album as a bandleader in 1978 and also worked as a studio guitarist with musicians such as Cat Stevens and Christopher Cross. His career took off in 1986 with his major label debut, Tones. In 1991, he won a Grammy for Best Rock Instrumental for "Cliffs of Dover," from his best-selling album Ah Via Musicom. *He continues to record, tour, and collaborate with other artists including Joe Satriani and Steve Vai.*

C Dorian Etude

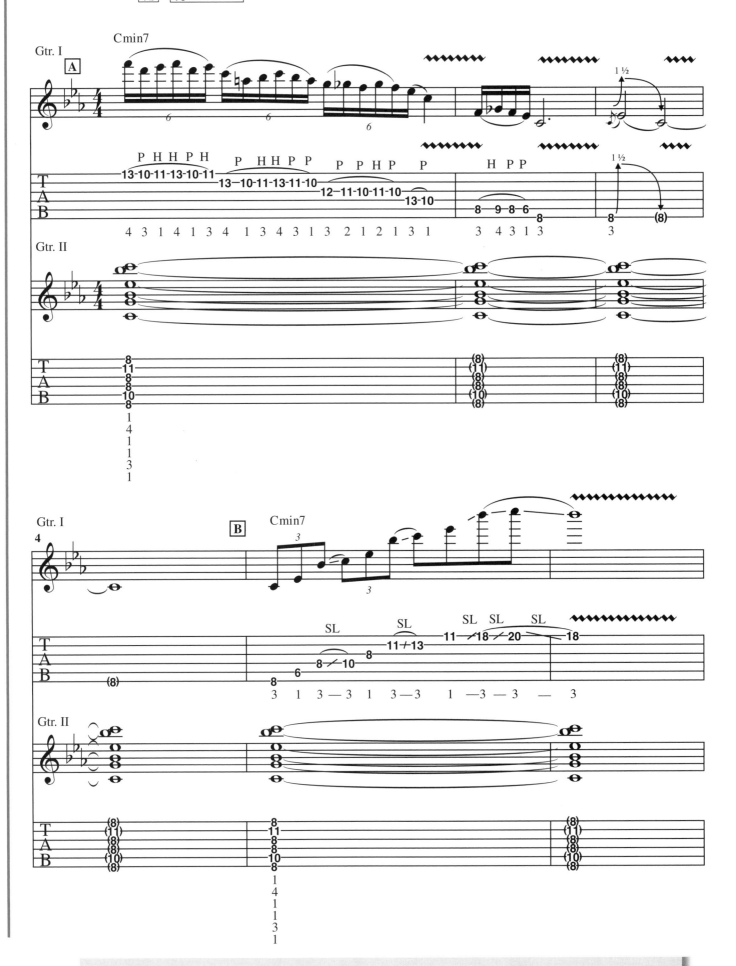

Congratulations! You made it to the end of the instructional portion of *Intelli-Shred*. Please continue through the last few sections for advice and pointers on the more cerebral and philosophical side of music. Hopefully, your newfound knowledge will put you on the path to finding your own unique voice in the world of music. Enjoy!

APPENDIX

A LISTENING EXERCISE

How well do you listen?

Okay, now how well do you think you *really* listen?

Try this little exercise:

1. First, put away your guitar. You won't be needing it.

2. Now, eliminate all outside distractions. Headphones will aid immensely in this process.

3. Choose a song that you don't mind listening to several times in a row. One of your all-time favorites should do.

4. To begin, just listen to the song as you always have. Think about what it is you enjoy about this particular piece of music.

5. Now, starting with the second listening, choose a particular voice or instrument (guitar, bass, keyboard, drums, background vocals, etc.) and try to listen only to what that particular voice is doing. Block everything else out with the exception of that one instrument or voice.

6. Now, repeat this process for every instrument or voice in your chosen song. Isolate each one, one at a time. By isolating all the different voices (human and instrumental), you'll come to better understand how all those different elements work together within the framework of this particular piece of music.

How are the different parts (instrument and vocal) orchestrated? Which part carries or establishes the mood, and how do the others support or enhance it?

A lot of the time, a great composition is like a house of cards. Each piece or part relies on and supports the others.

Now you might ask, "How does this have anything to do with playing the guitar?"

The first part of the answer is that you'll gain a greater awareness of how to arrange and orchestrate different parts in your writing. Secondly, understanding how all the parts come together helps you see that playing for the song—and not playing for your ego—is where true musicianship lies.

Chops are important, but knowing what *not* to play and when not to play are equally as important.

CHOOSING THE RIGHT TEACHER FOR YOU

There can be numerous reasons why a student fails or succeeds. Choosing the right teacher is an important part of the learning process. You should shop around for the best teacher to suit your needs as a student. It's also a good idea to interview prospective teachers (and for them to interview you) before you commit to lessons. You should openly discuss your goals as a guitarist along with the styles of music that interest you the most. There should be a connection made on some level, and ease of communication between the two of you is of extreme importance. Just like shopping for shoes or a great pair of jeans, you need to find the best fit for you.

It's a two way street; it's also in the teacher's best interest to enjoy working with the student. If things don't "click" between student and teacher, and no progress is being made, sometimes the teacher must let that student go. Conversely, an enthusiastic student can inspire the teacher to new heights. In this case, the lessons become a learning experience for the teacher as well.

Another thing to consider is that sometimes a student may outgrow an instructor. You may find yourself in a situation where you've both gone as far as you can with each other, or maybe the connection has been lost or things have become stale and stagnant. Here is where absolute honesty between student and teacher at all times is of the highest priority. A great teacher will not be afraid to tell a student "I've taken you as far as I can; now it's time to take off the training wheels so can you step out on your own."

Make sure the teacher you choose is familiar with the genres, styles, techniques, and artists that interest you. Most instructors can help you with the basics of playing, but it's just as important that your teacher can relate to your music.

***Michael Romeo** is best known as the founder and guitarist for Symphony X. Since 1994, their unique brand of progressive, neo-classical metal has attracted audiences all over the world. He is a master of many* Intelli-Shred *techniques such as sweep picking, tapping and string skipping. His solos are noted for their exotic scales, modes and rhythms. Michael has also released one solo recording entitled* The Dark Chapter.

SUGGESTIONS AND HELPFUL HINTS

- **Practice to your weaknesses/perform to your strengths.** Take the time to do self-assessments and always work towards a goal in your practice. A live performance isn't necessarily the best place and time to try something you've never attempted. While there's something to be said for letting it all hang out and going for broke, most extremely complex or technically-demanding music isn't improvised. It's usually very well rehearsed. Even the parts of a live show that appear completely over-the-top and out-of-control are often completely choreographed for your entertainment. You'll have to find your own balance between being a musician and being an entertainer.

- **Never perform with a new piece of gear.** Avoid taking a new piece out to a gig without first learning all its "ins and outs." Murphy's Law says that anything that *can* go wrong *will* go wrong. What will you do when your fancy piece of gear goes belly up in the middle of a gig, leaving you hanging?

- **Experiment with different sizes, gauges and styles of picks.** Your choice of pick can affect your tone as much as any other factor, such as the shapes of the calluses on your fingertips, the effects in your signal path, or the settings on your amp. There are many different materials out there and many different shapes. Try as many as you can. You probably spent hours picking out the perfect guitar and amp for yourself, so why not spend as much time on your choice of pick? Different thicknesses and different materials have different tones. Some materials are easier to grip than others. Different tip shapes have a different attack and release off the string, which could possibly add speed or even slow you down. The key is to experiment until you find the pick that's right for you.

- **Spend some of your practice time standing.** Things are a little different when the guitar isn't perfectly balanced right under your chin. Sometimes, you have to contort yourself to reach certain positions while playing in a standing position. When you think about it, you will probably play most of your gigs standing up, so you should spend some of your practice time standing up too.

- **Try practicing in front of a mirror.** The "practice mirror" concept can help you in many ways. Obviously, it can help you work on your cool rock star poses, or color-coordinating your outfit with your guitar, but that's not really what we're talking about here. When watching yourself practice in a mirror, you can take notice of things like: Are you wasting any movement? Are you keeping your hands close to the strings? Are you tensing up your forearm or shoulders when playing fast or demanding passages? Are you making smooth transitions or position shifts?

- **Spend some time and effort researching your favorite guitarist.** Find out as much as you can about your favorite guitarist. What gear does he use and why? Who are his favorite musicians to listen to and why? What scales or techniques does he rely on the most? The reasons for doing this are two-fold. First, as you gain more understanding about the player, you start to understand why he chooses particular sounds or licks and how he executes them. Second, by delving deeper into his influences, you may stumble across a new influence for yourself.

- **Keep a pair of nail trimmers with you.** Unfortunately, the more you play guitar, the more likely you are to develop some kind of fingernail issue. Keeping a pair of nail trimmers in your pocket or guitar case, along with your extra picks, is a great idea.

- **When gigging, try to have a backup for everything.** The stage is an unpredictable environment. If you gig enough, sooner or later something will break, die, fry, or go up in smoke. Bring more back-up gear than you think you'll need: picks, strings, batteries, cables, connectors, straps, tubes, fuses, etc. It's also a good idea to bring a small tool box and a flashlight in case you need to make an emergency repair.

- **Always be well-rehearsed and familiar with your material before a performance.** Practice at home or in your rehearsal space, not live in front of people. Nobody wants to pay big bucks to watch you struggle through an unfamiliar song. The more comfortable and familiar you are with your material, the more enjoyable your performance will be. When you're comfortable and relaxed, you have more fun, and your audience has more fun. They can see your enthusiasm shine from deep inside you.

- **Never leave for a big performance without doing an inventory to make sure you have everything you need.** This is especially important if you rely on charts for the songs. It's easy to forget a passage or little detail in the heat of the moment, and sometimes changes need to be made at the last minute due to time restrictions or other factors beyond your control. It's best to be ready for anything and everything. Thinking of every detail is what separates the professionals from the amateurs. In the world of professional music, reputation and reliability can make or break your career. If you have a reputation for being well-prepared, proficient and punctual, you'll have a much easier time getting gigs.

- **Listen to as much music as possible—even stuff you don't like.** "Now, why would I want to listen to something that I don't like?" you might ask. Well, first of all, maybe you've never listened to it before with a completely open and unprejudiced mind. Give it a second chance. Second, and most importantly, every type of music has something to teach you. Even a song you hate might have one element such as a lick or chord change that catches your attention. Take that element, learn it, and understand how and why it works. Then, bring that element back to your chosen style or genre. It might end up being the one thing that makes you stand out as a musician and separates you from the pack of guitarists playing the same licks over and over again.

- **Know the difference between being an "Ist" (or "Er") and being a musician.** Think about this for a moment: There are a great many talented singERs, guitarISTs, bassISTs and drummERs, but very few great *musicians*. "Ists" and "Ers" think only about themselves and their own egos. Musicians, on the other hand, live only for the moment and for the song. Being a great musician doesn't necessarily mean knowing all the theory, terms and "geek speak." Theory certainly helps you communicate with others, but it's not strictly required. Great musicians know that the music comes *through* them and not *because* of them.

RECOMMENDED READING FOR FURTHER STUDY

Matt Smith's Chop Shop for Guitar
by Matt Smith (National Guitar Workshop #07-1033)

Shred Is Not Dead
by Terry Syrek (Alfred/National Guitar Workshop #19324)

Progressive Rock Guitar
by Glenn Riley (Alfred/National Guitar Workshop #22547)

Mastering Rock Guitar
by Erik Halbig (Alfred/National Guitar Workshop #14096)

30 Day Guitar Workout
by Jody Fisher (Alfred/National Guitar Workshop #22894)

Rock Discipline
by John Petrucci (Alfred #25960)

John Petrucci's Wild Stringdom
edited and compiled by Askold Buk (Alfred #0349B)

Theory for the Contemporary Guitarist
by Guy Capuzzo (Alfred/National Guitar Workshop #16755)

NOTATION KEY

8va - -	**All'ottava.** Play the bracketed notes one octave higher than written.
Harm. ◇ 17	**Natural harmonic.** Lightly touch your left-hand finger on the string at the indicated fret. Do not press the string down onto the fret. When done correctly, this will create a high-pitched, ringing tone.
Art. Harm. ◇ XXIV **12**	**Artificial harmonic.** As with a natural harmonic, an artificial harmonic creates a high-pitched tone. Fret the string at the indicated fret with your left hand, and lightly touch the string with a right-hand finger at the fret indicated by the Roman numeral while you pick. If you do this at exactly the right spot, the harmonic will sound.
1	**Bend.** While maintaining pressure on the string with your left-hand finger, press or pull the string perpendicular to the neck so that the note goes up in pitch. The number above the arrow indicates how many steps the note should rise in pitch (half step, whole step, etc.).
1	**Bend and release.** Perform a bend (as described above), then release the bend so that the note returns to its original pitch while continuing to sustain.
0	**Divebomb.** Play the indicated note, then press down the whammy bar until the strings go completely loose, creating a "diving" sound. This technique sounds awesome with heavy distortion!
H 0 2	**Hammer-on.** Pick the first note normally, then "hammer" your left-hand finger onto the fret to sound the second note. Do not pick the second note with your right hand.
P.M. – – –	**Palm mute.** Rest the fleshy part of your picking hand against the strings for a punchy, muted sound.
P 2 0	**Pull-off.** Pick the first note normally, then pull your left-hand finger off the fret to sound the second note. Do not pick the second note with your right hand.
SL 14 — 16	**Slide.** While maintaining pressure on the string with your left-hand finger, slide your left hand up or down to the next note, resulting in a continuous sound.
T 9	**Tap.** Hammer-on to the indicated fret with your left-hand finger. Do not pluck the string with your right hand.
⌇⌇⌇	**Vibrato.** A series of small, quick bends that create a "singing" sound that fluctuates in pitch.

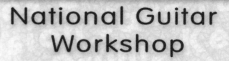